Danila Mayer

Park Youth in Vienna

Danila Mayer

Park Youth in Vienna

A Contribution to Urban Anthropology

LIT

This publication has been funded with support from the Austrian Federal Ministry of Science and Research (BM:WF), the federal state government of Vorarlberg (Amt der Vorarlberger Landesregierung) and the cultural department of Vienna (Kulturabeilung der Stadt Wien - MA 7).

Bibliographic information published by the Deutsche Nationalbibliothek
The Deutsche Nationalbibliothek lists this publication in the Deutsche Nationalbibliografie; detailed bibliographic data are available in the Internet at http://dnb.d-nb.de.

ISBN 978-3-643-50253-7

A catalogue record for this book is available from the British Library

©LIT VERLAG GmbH & Co. KG Wien 2011
Krotenthallergasse 10/8
A-1080 Wien
Tel. +43 (0) 1-409 56 61
Fax +43 (0) 1-409 56 97
e-Mail: wien@lit-verlag.at
http://www.lit-verlag.at

LIT VERLAG Dr. W. Hopf
Berlin 2011
Fresnostr. 2
D-48159 Münster
Tel. +49 (0) 2 51-620 320
Fax +49 (0) 2 51-922 60 99
e-Mail: lit@lit-verlag.de
http://www.lit-verlag.de

Distribution:
In Germany: LIT Verlag Fresnostr. 2, D-48159 Münster
Tel. +49 (0) 2 51-620 32 22, Fax +49 (0) 2 51-922 60 99, e-mail: vertrieb@lit-verlag.de
In Austria: Medienlogistik Pichler-ÖBZ, e-mail: mlo@medien-logistik.at

In the UK: Global Book Marketing, e-mail: mo@centralbooks.com

Contents

Acknowledgements

Thanks to all who let me share the park life.

My gratitude goes to Professor Ghaus Ansari, who introduced me to urban anthropology and to studies of the Windy City, and to Andre Gingrich, who supported me on long and winding roads.

I want to thank all my former youth and streetwork colleagues, and the Verein Wiener Jugendzentren.

People who helped with the final version of the book are Muzaffer Hasaltay, Onur Serdar, Roland Fischer-Briand, Craig Crossen, Maziar and Meisam Varahram, and Ercan Yalcinkaya.

Park, Urban Loritz Platz

Introduction

This study aims at introducing the park youth of Vienna in their world. It presents the peer groups, their spatial contexts within the neighborhoods and the city, and their social contexts at work, with families, and at school; and it takes into account their situation as youth in present-day cities, coming of age in the global urban society.

Adolescence is a universal human experience. Adolescents have their particular social structures and their specific views, and they must be perceived as a distinct group. But growing up in urban surroundings entails special conditions.

Adolescents are lively, dynamic, and hungry for experience. This ethnography contributes to a global view of the special conditions under which adolescence, as a cognitive-physiological developmental stage, takes place today. From my long-time activities as a youth worker in Vienna, I know that park-based adolescents are marginalized in Viennese society, and increasingly threatened by further exclusion through economic shifts connected to globalization, and international conflicts and crises. Enabling them to express their views, experiences, and approaches to life through bringing them onto the stage of research is an attempt to strengthen their position, and to increase awareness of the criticism of urban society implicit in the very existence of such de-linked groups.

Research Questions

Adolescents lacking other resources use parks to meet others, to communicate, and to find support and emotional reinforcement. Parks and public space are important zones of learning for the young.

I had long observed that adolescents form quite stable groups in the parks. Which group formation processes can be found? What types of groups can be discerned, and how do such groups grow and change? What about the girls?

One of my questions has been how the characteristics of park life are connected with the majority society that often excludes but yet surrounds these youth. Where and how do youth groups from parks interact with society at-large?

Many adolescents in parks share an immigrant background. Their friendship groups are often "ethnically" mixed, and Vienna's adolescents may have more in common with each other than with their parents. It can be a methodological problem to research adolescents as members of their descendant families and ethnic communities. So what experiences do these young people have with life in Vienna, and how do these relate to their parents'? How about "back home"?

Park youth in Vienna are coming of age in urban surroundings: What experiences in and with the city do they have, and in what special way can their growing-up be said to be "urban"?

The processes of globalization inevitably influence young people. But in what specific ways does this happen? How do economic and other global processes shape their lives; and how are Vienna's park adolescents in particular linked to the world?

And finally, while communication and the mutual exchange of knowledge between researcher and park groups are part of the ethnographic experience, the flip side is the ethnographer's attempt to articulate the studied groups' views inside academia. I wanted to see how the park youth's ethnography would fit anthropology.

Overview of the Study

In the first part, Coming of Age in the Global Metropolis, an examination of the concepts of puberty, adolescence, youth, and adulthood is followed by an introduction to growing up in cities. My research on youth also uses concepts from urban anthropology.

Literature on Chicago, London and Paris has enabled me to place youth in Vienna as a social phenomenon into a larger picture. The classical ethnographic studies of the Chicago School from the 1920's are relevant both for youth research and urban anthropology. Metropolitan youth in London is presented through the works of Paul Gilroy, Helena Wulff, and Gerd Baumann. A specific interest has been to ascertain the present state of research on youth and adolescents in social and cultural anthropology in Vienna, and, more particularly, the study of young Viennese in anthropology and other disciplines. Considerations on urban space and landscape, on Victor Turner's concept of the arena, and on groups close the first part.

At the Café: Jahangir, Dane, Suela, Sarah, Gina, and Ilhan rest from photo shooting
"Frieden und Krieg". October 2004

The second part of the book, "We're Doing It in the Park!" is my ethnography of park adolescents in Vienna[1]. This section comprises the parks as arena; and park youth in their spatial and social contexts.

The Arena introduces the parks as ethnographic research areas in the larger context of Vienna. After the description of the relevant neighborhood parks, the adolescents are discussed in their group formations. Additional ethnographic material follows in the chapter on Bodies; and the increasingly diffi- cult conditions park-based adolescents must deal with are described from the standpoint of older adolescents and young adults.

In Spatial and Social Contexts, I follow the park groups into their city neighborhoods, which also includes park adolescents' uses of the internet and television. Other places they frequent are situated in the common urban areas. I observe their experiences with jobs and at work. Young park users are briefly shown in their families, their transnational experiences, and their political atti- tudes. Some observations of park kids at school close the ethnographic section.

---

1   The title comes from the Blackbyrds' song "Rock Creek Park" from the album *City Life* (Fantasy 1975): "We're doing it in the park, we're doing it after dark …".

Finally, the empirical results are summarized and discussed in the contexts of my research questions, of the adolescents' growing up in the global urban society, and of the background studies and literature.

Methodology

My ethnography is based on long-term participant observation, and includes a vast amount of data collected over many years. Additional background comes from my earlier transnational field study (1994). The material and data in the present book were predominantly, but not exclusively, obtained during my years as a youth worker, and I have taken the opportunity to bring the experiences and findings of my daily streetwork into the international academic discourse.

Researching existing groups in their settings by doing long-term fieldwork involves looking at what people do while hearing what they say. In addition to the informal talks and daily observations, in 2003 and 2005 I did detailed interviews as anthropological data collections on "Young Urban Migrants Between Two Cultures", and on health issues among marginalized adolescents[2]. I had been acquainted with the interviewees for many years, and we enjoyed a relationship of mutual trust that included many shared experiences. Therefore the results of the interviews could be evaluated taking the adolescents' background into consideration. A short field study in the summer of 2009 provided new data on urban park youths' internet uses.

For the present book, I have also taken into account some of my friends' own reminiscences of their park times during their earlier years, and their years after park life. Younger acquaintances have supplied fresh information, as the generational change in the parks has been quite rapid.

However, collecting data on adolescents' daily lives, practices, ideas, experiences, and troubles in the context of youth work implies several specific methodological considerations.

---

2   For this I interviewed 9 adolescents between ages 17 and 20. My work led to cooperation with medical student Benjamin Schindlauer who got interested in adolescents' health. Schindlauer conducted interviews with 12 (younger) adolescents in parks (2006–8). His relevant diploma work was completed in 2008.

Youth Work, Streetwork, Crisis Intervention

Vienna's community-funded youth work, a corollary of Austria's status as one of Europe's welfare states, has developed diverse approaches to the thousands of urban adolescents who lack resources. Aimed at providing support to these youths, centers have been opened up offering space to the young where they can spend time together and with adult youth workers; and numerous adolescent groups are contacted in public space by streetworkers. Strong relationships have been established, providing a communication bridge where information and knowledge flow in both directions. This is necessary for offering support on the one hand, and for relaying the adolescents' demands, needs, and implicit or explicit criticisms to decision makers, politicians, and the city administration.

Youth work is not performed for the purpose of obtaining scientific knowledge, but for the purposes of general support and immediate crisis intervention, socio-political lobbying, and developing conditions and structures where adolescents can present their positions, participate in decisions, and eventually, are heard.

Therefore, the adolescents were supported as far as possible both in acute crisis and in a general way during data collection: their situation generally improved and in any case, they were not left on their own. The researcher's agency is thus implicitly included in the observations as well. In order to fully understand the adolescents, seeing them not as defined by problems and defects, but as resourceful persons, the information obtained is of a definitely ethnographic nature. However, certain youth activities did not take place and/or were not directly observed because the presence of the researcher/youth worker discouraged them, but on the other hand, several activities and the ensuing shared experiences were initiated by youth workers, and would most probably not have happened without them.

The activities and lobbying which were part of my own work are the *Petition Jugendlich – schuldlos – papierlos* (petition for youth without documents, 1998 onwards), the photo project *Frieden und Krieg* (Peace and War), which brought together park youth from the 5th District with young refugees and undocumented migrants who stayed at the Traiskirchen refugee camp (2004); and the literature collection *Parkgeschichten* (2006), which has 23 texts and poems written by youth on park benches and under trees.

Most of my ethnographic data comes from informal talks with hundreds of adolescents between the ages of ten or eleven and twenty-four, and participant observation with and among youths met in parks. The parks in the 5th District where most of my interactions and observations took place are: Bacherpark, Einsiedlerpark, Hundsturmpark, Lichtblau-Park, Schütte-Lihotzky Park, Hartmannpark, Hochhauspark, Bruno Kreisky Park, Siebenbrunnenplatz, and numerous smaller grounds (Geheimpark, Bärlipark). Youth work activities and organized events for adolescents (media, music, politics, sports) also took my colleagues and me to parks in Districts 10, 11, 16, 17, and 20.

Once a relationship with an adolescent group had been established in public space, they often invited us youth workers to join them at other meeting places where they went, clubs, discotheques, and cafés. But our presence and support were also sought by youths who had to face police appointments and court trials. Visits in detention units and in crisis intervention centers were part of our work as well.

Furthermore, for years I enjoyed the company of numerous park adolescents at our youth work office in Vienna's 5th District, which became a much-favored hangout for park kids in groups, and on their own. We often sat together, chatted and talked, had coffee and cooked, and sometimes celebrated together. The data also include the results of 159 survey questionnaires (Mayer/ Möderndorfer 1998). Another background to this study is the analysis and in-

Frieden und Krieg: flyer, 2004

terpretation of quantitative data (frequency in public space, age, and gender) from the 1997 to 2006 annual reports of Back on Stage[3].

Youth work in the parks also provided glimpses into the lives of adolescents who were already involved in more harmful and dangerous practices. These observations prompted us to take a stronger interest in groups and individuals who had left the parks to pursue careers in hard drugs[4].

---

3   Back on Stage, in this case in the 5th District, is part of the community-funded Verein Wiener Jugendzentren. Information, reports and publications from them are available at www.jugendzentren.at and www.mobilejugendarbeit.at.

4   We researched the adolescents' and young adults' drug scenes in 1999 as a joint project with Vienna's drug streetworkers (Verein Wiener Sozialprojekte), and conducted in-depth interviews with more than fifty adolescents and young adults.

Meeting point: central library

I. Coming of Age

in the

Global Metropolis

1. Growing Up

Puberty and the Expansion of the Mind

Puberty, the period of the biological processes maturing a person's ability to procreate, is a universal human experience. The original Latin *pubertas* alludes to the activity of the genital organs. Their development is instigated by increased hormone production, a process connected with the corresponding growth and reorganization of parts of the brain. There is still very little knowledge about these processes and we need to be wary of generalizing findings from Western industrialized societies, but it seems that a profound brain re-structuring takes place, enhancing the ability to understand life in a more complex manner, what I would call "expansion of the mind". Involved are moral judgement, reflexivity, and a fresh evaluation of the world and its inhabitants. This at least partially explains teenagers' new approach to life manifesting itself in alienation, and prompts a period of self-invention and new positioning. Included are the questioning of adult behavior and the criticism, and often ridicule, of parents, teachers, police, and other authority figures.

Puberty is the bodily manifestation of the irreversible transition from child into an adult. Apart from that biological process, the other transformations – emotional, cognitive, social – are often subsumed as adolescence.

Adolescence

Adolescence derives from the Latin *adolescere*, which refers to growing (up), and also growing into social adulthood. Evolutionist adolescence researcher Stanley Hall understood adolescence as a "new birth" (Hall 1904:xiii), but adolescence is more often perceived as a time of adjustment, of settling into the adult world, of beginning to take on the responsibilities of adult life after leaving childhood.

In their *Adolescence. An Anthropological Enquiry* (which will be discussed in more detail below) cultural anthropologists A. Schlegel and H. Barry say:

An anthropological definition of adolescence, in common with psychological and sociological definitions, recognizes adolescence as a social stage intervening between childhood and adulthood in the passage through life. ... Adolescence can be seen as a period of social role learning and restructuring: not simply a period in which early learning is crystallized, but rather one in which unlearning and new learning take place (Schlegel and Barry 1991:8).

Youth

Youth is another term referring to not-yet adults. Schlegel and Barry define it as the stage between adolescence and adulthood when "full social adulthood is delayed many years beyond puberty" (1991:10). They explain: "In most societies, adulthood follows adolescence, but in a minority there is a youth stage before full adulthood is reached". They find this youth stage "to be most common in traditional or modern states" (1991:35).

Youth sociologist Natalia Wächter observes that the term "youth" got its modern meaning only at the end of the 19th century, "following the establishment of modern industrial society and in context with the effect of the bourgeois family model. The meaning of 'youth' thus depends on the respective society and the historical instant" (Wächter 2006:125; translated by DM).

Youth researchers Lothar Böhnisch and Wolfgang Schröer argue that 21st century digital capitalism is also in need of a new social form "youth" (2007:173). But this new form is still unknown, a chimera.

Experience and the Body as Medium

I take adolescence to be a period of new experiences profoundly changing a person's outlook. Such experiences include those with one's own and others' bodies, with peers, and with political and social structures of society at-large. The physiological and cognitive processes, brought about by the restructuring of the brain and the expansion of the mind, result in a new view of self and an enhanced responsiveness to the external world.

Adolescence seems to be a collective journey towards an unknown destination. It is a transformation process, and its heterogeneous experiences are primary inputs into a changing body-mind-matrix, the interplay of body, mind-expansion, and emotions, intensified by communication and exchange with other people. The body is both the medium by which, as well as the screen upon which these processes are played. Biological changes and functions are projected into society where they are recognized: one's growing up is visible to all.

Medical anthropologists N. Scheper-Hughes and M. Lock assume the body as "simultaneously a physical and symbolic artefact, as both naturally and culturally produced, and as securely anchored in a particular historical moment" (Scheper-Hughes and Lock 1998:208). Brain development, the mind, consciousness, behavior, and the body must not be viewed separately but thought of as aspects of the same unity. But the body is also transient, in that by sharing emotions and affects with others, it dissolves in joy, ecstasy, or resistance. The intersubjective nature of affect, which is "essentially a pre-personal category, installed 'before' the circumscription of identities" (Guattari 1990:66), enables the affective mode of communication, which can become "a door to a singular yet collective experience" (Kato 2007:5).

Fragmented Initiations

In classical ethnology and the cultural anthropology of pre-industrial groups and societies, the *rites de passages* (Van Gennep 1909) connected to puberty usually mark the transition from childhood into adulthood. According to the cross-cultural adolescence researchers Alice Schlegel and Herbert Barry, the corresponding initiation ceremonies are mainly aimed at strengthening gender identity (see also H. Barry on "Initiation Rites", *Encyclopedia of Cultural Anthropology*, 1996).

In present-day society, demarcation of age and status is vague and ill-defined. Feminist sociologist Cornelia Helfferich, in her *Jugend, Körper und Geschlecht* (1994), sees various strategies, "imaginary solutions", adolescents use to cope with their difficulties in growing up. A stretched (extended or prolonged) youth is prevalent among middle class kids in higher education; and a shortened youth is found among working class youth through early identification with work and jobs for boys, and early sexual initiation for girls. In her ethnographic approach, Helfferich uses the concept of "Teil-Initiationen" (partial initiations) to discern the various processes that run parallel in adolescence.

Definition and symbolic meaning of behavior are produced as interaction in a specific context, negotiated among adolescents, and between adolescents and parents or other adults. Problems of coping are met collectively as adolescents put attempts with each other on stage to solve their developmental tasks, e.g. the searching for and testing of a sexual identity (Helfferich 1994:193f.). This behavior is embedded in adolescents' interactions, and an active performance. We do not simply grow into something! Young people take over and change the social rules for bodily practices with their own and other people's bodies (Helfferich 1994:49). Their invention of self-initiations, partial initiations, and rites include work initiation, sexual initiation, and accompanying initiations in body practices.

For my ethnography, I prefer to speak of *fragmented* initiations: fractured into a multitude of initial experiences in sexual development, love and parenthood, work and leisure time activities, responsibilities, and more.

Adulthood and Definition of Adolescence

Apart from the biological fact of the accomplished personal physical maturity (Lat. *adultus*), the attainment of adulthood is rather elusive, there is no role continuity where adolescents take on the adult roles of their parents on clear paths into adulthood ("Adolescence", *The Social Science Encyclopedia*, 2004). In the present-day, global and urbanized society, the end of childhood is still more or less obvious from the physiological changes brought about by puberty; but the promised or expected "arrival" at adulthood as the end of adolescence does not happen so easily.

Adulthood is an ambiguous term that requires definition. If understood as comprising full participation in society – including integration in the job world and the establishment of a family –, adulthood might for many people not occur at all, as education, work, and family foundation tend to be postponed or only partially accomplished, and are not necessarily linked. Other, sometimes

Young public at the Street Parade, 1997

nominally "adult" activities and responsibilities (work, marriage, childbearing) are incurred earlier, even in childhood. We find the phenomena of denied childhoods, a shortening of the period called youth, and an indefinitely prolonged social adolescence. As fragmented experiences in different spheres of life are the rule, specific markers of adulthood are lacking.

The period of adolescence is therefore here defined as determined by the young people themselves: it starts when they begin consciously distancing themselves from childhood, and extends to the time they speak about themselves as a grown-up. Depending on their personal circumstances, they might spend most of their time in the park before and after feeling adolescent.

2. The Global Urban Society

a. Cities

More than half of the world's young people experience their adolescence in cities, mega cities, metropolises, megalopolises, urban conglomerates, and the "oecumenopolis"[5], and all the world's adolescents are in any case part of the global urbanized society.

Urban is a term for all such settlements since the "urban revolution" roughly 10,000 years ago, an expression introduced by archaeologist V. Gordon Childe. Ansari and Nas say that Childe "saw the shift from small scale settlement patterns to large urban sites as a basic change in human history, which he referred to as the 'urban revolution', related to a shift in economic productivity" (Ansari and Nas 1983:2). The shift in economic productivity is related to the emergence of urban classes, and Aidan Southall, in his seminal work *The City in Time and Space*, states that the city is "the central arena on which the fateful drama of human wealth and inequality has been played" (Southall 2000:14). Today's global society is thoroughly urbanized. "In late capitalist economies the influence of the city penetrates the remotest places to such an extent that they become in a sense urban" (Southall 2000:7).

Most of the young urbanites who are the subjects of this study belong to the property-less urban population. Poverty is not exclusively an urban phenomenon of course, but cannot be neglected, along with density of the environment, activities, communication, and aesthetic sensibility, "all necessarily correlated with parallel processes of the division of labour, role differentiation and increasing inequality" (Southall 2000:4). Cities are marked by a "concentration of social relationships", the "most fundamental characteristic common to cities in all time and space" (Southall 2000:9)

---

5   Term used by Southall (2000). Southall explained earlier: "One form of concentration is megalopolis, or ecumenopolis, propounded by Gottman (1961), Doxiadis and Papaioannon (1968) and Toynbee (1970)." (Southall 1983:19).

Cities can hardly be viewed only as malevolent, the cause of poverty, suffering, and anonymity. It is the duality of urban conglomerates, the ambiguity involved in cities, which "have given expression to the best and the worst extremes of human potentiality" (Southall 2000:4). Adolescents as persons with new experiences and outlooks are among those who can contribute their potential to urban life and to a city's development. But urban adolescents' lives are also connected with global processes.

b. Urban Adolescents and Globalization Processes

Which processes of globalization are especially relevant for young people? There are economic factors, but also aesthetic, emotional, and political influences to be taken into account, as well as the worldwide web and global popular culture, especially music, and a globally homogenizing consumer culture.

Global Economy, and the Universe of Work

Pierre Bourdieu holds that the economic habitus, based on rational action theory, is not at all a general human way of thinking, but is historically produced; pre-capitalist economies do not have a set of constituted and independent economic practices (Bourdieu 2000:7f.). Economy is embedded in society. Eric Wolf speaks of the "penetration of capitalism, the growth of a worldwide specialization and division of labor, and the development of domination by some populations over others" (Wolf 2010:15). Some acute processes in the globalization of the world economy are: a decreasing number of national economies; de-industrialization in wealthy Western countries and the corresponding shift of production "to poor countries defenceless against pollution and labour exploitation"; and "the Japanese option" of automation and high technology (Southall 2000:412).

While Vienna is not one of the global cities from which control of the "global assembly line" (Sassen 2001:10) is exercised, its economic production is still part of this globalized economy. The shift away from local production, manufacturing, and industry towards increasing global trading and post-industrial services-based sectors has had its impact.

Asking about this impact of the new economic structures on adolescents, sociologists A. Oehme, C. Beran, and R. Krisch (2007) worked with Viennese adolescent groups from the poorer social strata. The researchers present an analysis of the situation and problems working-class adolescents face in today's Vienna, from structural changes in work to problems of social integration into adulthood. Their data show that many adolescents' transfer into working life is fragmented, fractured, depends more and more on personal networks, experiences and social skills, and is in no way easy or automatic. This contributes to the other factors making these young people vulnerable to economic exclusion.

Periods of unemployment and underemployment are interwoven with funded support courses and involuntary periods of leisure. The increased fragmentations of biographies around the youths' entry into the realm of work persist far into adulthood. The sad paradox is that, because of the change from industrial capitalism to a "flexible Arbeitsgesellschaft" (flexible labor society), there is a waning job market at the very time that jobs and work are most desired by youth (Oehme/Beran/Krisch 2007:45f.). This is impressively confirmed by the authors' empirical data from interviews with Viennese youth workers, and the adolescents who they try to support. In addition, few jobs are permanent or secure for a longer period. It is not possible to "grow into the job".

Work, as a sense-provider and meaning-giver, is increasingly lacking in adolescents' lives, and they have to deal with a growing distance from that universe. Adolescents must try to come to terms without the inclusion in the work force, without the experiences of solidarity, pride in strength and abilities, the specific forms of sociability connected with industrial labor, and without participation in political movements emerging from the factories.

As work is not easily available, adolescents' subjectivity is marked by their feelings of uselessness, and of being superfluous. And *if* work finally, and often suddenly materializes, after long-term "careers" as job seekers, it will dramatically alter daily life, and needs to be somehow or the other integrated. As Fabrice Plomb maintains in his "Jugendliche – allergisch gegen Arbeit?", everything must be newly structured around work, their "Alltag und was er mit sich bringt, seine Gewohnheiten, seine Ordnung und seine Träume" ("everyday life and what it brings, its habits, its order and its dreams", Plomb 2001:62). Adolescents develop the strategies of a "straw in a river" – that is, soft, or weak, strategies of flexibility (2001:64ff.). In that, long-time planning is not possible, neither are self-education, or exercising one's skills, since to what end, in what direction, for which use is not assessable.

In his contribution to *Der Lohn der Angst*, Fabrice Plomb cites Pierre Bourdieu who – ever exposing false promises and illusions of equal opportunity – says that the economic and social worlds form a marked-off universe which is full of orders and restrictions, signs of acquisition and exclusion, compulsory meanings, and insurmountable obstacles. This universe is deeply fragmented, "un univers balisé" (Bourdieu 1997:267).

World Politics and Transnational Linkages

The adolescents who we will meet in this study come of age in surroundings where a variety of geo-political processes touch their lives.

The new Republic of Austria became a sovereign state in 1955 after the active participation in the Third Reich. Labor immigration started soon after, predominantly with recruited workers[6] from Turkey and Yugoslavia, countries that had had historic relations with the Habsburg Empire through Austria's imperial connections with the Ottoman Empire, and her engagement in the Balkans.

Saskia Sassen (1995) analysed how migration-sending and migration-receiving countries are connected through transnational linkages which are understated in the debate, such as the formation of subjective and objective bridges between the countries (including transnational households and kinship structures). Countries usually receive immigrants from their historical zones of influence (Sassen 1995:24). As globalization proceeds, transnationality of economy leads to more linkages and increased migration flows. The migration-sending countries are strongly affected by population loss and cannot "catch up in terms of development with those areas that emerge as labor importing areas", and their local economic structures tend to disintegrate under the stress of emigration (Sassen 1995:11f.).

As a further point of view, European societies can be analysed in their postcolonial contexts. A. Gingrich and M. Banks explain in *Neo-Nationalism in Europe and Beyond*, how the "dethroned" former colonial powers are "in the process of aggressively readjusting themselves to new immigrant generations from the realms of their former colonial subjects" (Gingrich and Banks 2006:9). And although Austria has not been one of the big colonial powers, such conditions seem not too far off[7].

In her article "French Suburbia 2005: The Return of the Politically Unrecognized", philosopher Rada Ivekovic sees the *banlieu* youth uprisings as exposing the unresolved colonial past (2008). She describes the suburban rioters as "[v]ery macho boys deprived of any material or language capital, of any material goods or instruments, poor in emotions, gender relations and political knowledge". For Ivekovic, the riots were connected to the colonial past, and not to current immigration. Most of the rioters, whose parents come from diverse backgrounds, "have been French for one or more generations, so how much longer will they be considered immigrants?" France's de-colonization

---

6   On these processes and the role of the unions see especially Eveline Wollner (1996).
7   Recent literature on Austria's coloniality is Davis-Sulikowski and Khittel (2004).

Pilgramgasse/Wienzeile

needs yet to be accomplished, because the "renegotiation of a new and political project for postcolonial metropolitan France" is still lacking (Ivekovic
2008:173ff.)[8].

Another influence on adolescents connected to globalization as well is neo-
nationalism, which Gingrich and Banks specify as the "re-emergence of nationalism under different global and transnational conditions" (Gingrich and
Banks 2006:2). Such conditions include the nationalist wars in Yugoslavia and
also presently in the Caucasus, which have brought many refugees to Austria.

---

8   Additionally, it is interesting to view the riots in Parisian *banlieus* as constituting an "are-
     na" in Victor Turner's sense: "for a regime that has lost legitimacy the arena might be the
     streets of the city" (1994:135). A social drama in such an arena starts with a breach or
     non-fulfilment of crucial norms (1994:38) – in the case in question, the (presumed?)
     killing of two boys by the police.

Check den Park! Streetball 1997

Bodies

Globalized influences on the adolescents' body images and their physical existence are strong. Adolescents are target groups of especially aggressive global marketing particularly for tobacco and alcohol products. They are also vulnerable to severe health damage and to accidents, suicides, and homicides (the three major causes of adolescents' death in the USA according to *The New York Times, 2007*). Health risks include hazardous jobs, often in the black market and the informal sector; violence; poor nutrition; and traffic, air pollution, dogs, and the generally bad living circumstances associated with urban conglomerates.

Young people are also especially and distinctly targeted by marketing strategies directly aimed at influencing and accessing the body image, which, according to medical anthropologists Scheper-Hughes and Lock, "refers to the collective and idiosyncratic representations an individual entertains about the body in its relationship to the environment, including internal and external perceptions, memories, affects, cognitions, and actions" (Scheper-Hughes and Lock 1998:208).

Mariahilfer Strasse, 10/2010

The constantly renewed imperatives of mass consumption increasingly aim at a person's body and the way one should look like, perform, and feel, and what input should be taken. The glorification of fitness, bodily strength, beauty, and health, and a "body-fication" of identity take place, and this is a direct influence on young people's body images. Emotions and feelings are likewise inseparable from such concepts, and globalization is "the latest stage of colonization, not only in terms of territorial, economic, and political domination but also in terms of the domination over imagery and aesthetics" (Kato 2007:3)[9].

But body images are not solely determined by blind consumerism and globally streamlined aesthetics. Styles are creatively produced and express feelings, attitudes, and political positions. As an example from ethnographic fieldwork, Helena Wulff shows in her study of *Twenty Girls*[10] how they had

---

9   Scholar and activist M. T. Kato here refers to colonization in the context of the penetration of the unconscious, as Frederic Jameson uses it (Jameson, F., 1991, *Postmodernism, or, the Cultural Logic of Late Capitalism*. Durham: Duke University Press, p. 36).

10 Wulff, Helena (1988), *Twenty Girls*. Stockholm Studies in Social Anthropology, no. 21, Stockholm: Department of Social Anthropology, Stockholm University.

incorporated their anti-racist attitudes into their bodily styles. These were "a formative experience that will be useful for them in the long run as they go on dealing with multi-cultural England" (Wulff 1995:77).

Such interplay between incorporated experiences and youth styles, impressions and expressions, is important when inquiring about the global influences on adolescents.

Global Popular Culture

Global popular culture is a homogenized and mainstream-lined, heavily marketed and mediated business, pursued by globally active enterprises. Clothes, make-up, and lifestyles are propagated and advertised by stars and celebrities. For popular youth culture a main medium is music, and especially, black popular music. Black music has been the accompaniment for resistance and protest movements; and it has given people a sense of self-worth, the expression of creativity, transcendence, and affective communication.

But economic exclusion may turn youth culture into a merely residual and reactive pseudo-option, as shown in Livio Sansone's study, "The making of a black youth culture" (1995).

Sansone discusses young men of Surinamese origin in Amsterdam, who are excluded from middle class and mainstream society in post-migration and post-colonial conditions. Their prolonged adolescence is due to unemployment in the official labor market, and adult life becomes their entrenchment in youth cultural styles and pastimes financed by drug-peddling. Sansone's study is long-term, and we meet men in their forties who still adhere to this lifestyle. Their identification with being black, and with black music (reggae), masks their exclusion from urban mainstream only superficially, while they are paradoxically integrated and marginalized at the same time: "Mainstream urban culture is incorporating many black symbols. ... In the meantime black people are marginal to the centres of production and power" (Sansone 1995:138).

Global popular culture also has this ambiguity to it, and may be seen as positioned between creative experience and exclusion mechanisms. The planet-wide access to music, movies, video games, music clips, inexpensive telecommunication, and the innumerable possibilities of interactivity on a worldwide scale[11] must be analysed along this duality. New forms of grouping and peer life –

---

11   These new structures are the basis for what Masahide Kato called, referring to Kung Fu and hiphop, a "popular cultural revolution" (2007).

Flyer Strictly Street Heroes # 5(1998): Michael Jordan

"technosociality"[12] – develop in virtual realities, as people make (virtual) friends around the globe; and new possibilities to circulate self-created information and knowledge evolve. People and groups use this potential as an enhanced main-streaming and consumer-orientation, and also in practices of resistance.

---

12   "... technosociality, a process of socio-cultural construction activated by the new tech-
     nologies" (Budka and Kremser 2004:213). The authors refer to Arturo Escobar's article
     Welcome to Cyberia (1994), in Current Anthropology 35 (3), pp. 211–231.

3. Adolescents in Research

a. Adolescence in the History of Cultural Anthropology

There are two studies I wish to discuss here: Margaret Mead's ethnographic work in Samoa, and Schlegel/Barry's cross-cultural analysis of pre-industrial adolescence. These works about adolescence and youth in cultural anthropology inform on pre-industrial societies both from a fieldwork and from an historical perspective.

Coming of Age: Margaret Mead

Margaret Mead, firmly rooted in cultural anthropology, studied puberty and adolescence as human universals in a relatively homogeneous society, and combined it with research in and of US American settings.

When Margaret set out for the South Seas in 1925 to study adolescent girls in a village in Samoa, her own adolescent years were barely over. Sent by her PhD advisor Franz Boas to find information on girls, it was her own idea to go to Polynesia. She worked with more than 60 girls, collecting data on their body, sexuality, group life, and more[13]. She included these findings into a village ethnography which she published in 1928, *Coming of Age in Samoa*, her first volume of the South Seas trilogy. The book was a success, perhaps most importantly among a non-scientific public, people who obviously wanted information about sexuality in exotic places.

Mead found that adolescence held no special stress for the Samoan girls in Ta'u, but that they easily grew into an adulthood characterized by a multiplicity of options for conflict reduction. Mead stated that adolescence was not a difficult period for them because "no one feels very strongly" (Mead 1936:200).

---

13   Derek Freeman, in his chapter "Mead's Samoan Fieldwork in Retrospect", maintains that Mead had only about 10 weeks for her fieldwork with adolescent girls (Freeman 1999:153).

These views can hardly be inferred from the material she presented. For example, she observed that the boys and girls in a household strictly avoided each other (Mead 1936:44), and that the "first attitude which a little girl learns towards boys is one of avoidance and antagonism" (Mead 1936:86). Mead does not explain how this strict avoidance among girls and boys could change into the light-hearted adolescent sexual relationships, without jealousy and other problems, she describes. Also, the young people's sexual relationships do not seem to have been as generally accepted as Mead says, given the fact that young people were expected to be in their very own beds – alone – in the morning. Mead instead gives the description of what sounds like a rigid patriarchal society, stressing the importance of virginity with the institution of the *tautou* (the village virgin), and requiring girls to work and to look after their younger siblings as soon as they can walk themselves. Her charts on girls in the appendix give sparse data, and are not helpful for understanding the girls' emotions, feelings, and experiences in growing up.

However, Mead used her findings to criticize US-American social institutions of adolescence and their needless stress. She attributed this to the ambiguities adolescents were dealt by the dominant culture: "our children are faced with half a dozen standards of morality" (Mead 1936:201), and Mead urged that "children must be taught how to think not what to think" (1936:246).

Adolescence. An Anthropological Enquiry: Alice Schlegel and Herbert Barry

Providing an ample historical survey of adolescence in pre-industrial societies, A. Schlegel and H. Barry collected and analysed 186 pre-industrial society samples of the human universal adolescence for cross-cultural research. However, the cases "represent a world that has vanished" (Schlegel/Barry 1991:200).

Adolescence, a "social stage in all human societies, intervening between non-reproductive childhood and reproductive adulthood" (Schlegel/Barry 1991:198), is "a response to sexual development in humans. Social recognition is given to the growth of reproductive capacity as marking the end of childhood and the prelude to adult life" (Schlegel/Barry 1991:207f.).

The objective of their cross-cultural study is the search for a "universal or nearly universal stage of social adolescence" and on their central tenets is that there is a "measurable difference ... between the treatment of girls and that of boys, corresponding to a universal distinction between the sexes in social roles and cultural perception" (Schlegel/Barry 1991:12). Schlegel/Barry, referring to research in child development, ethology, and primatology, believe the basic reason for the social arrangements connected to adolescence (e.g. peer groups) to be the avoidance of close inbreeding.

For adolescence in modernizing societies – those in contact with "Western" societies – Schlegel/Barry find a common feature that "almost everywhere, adolescents are learning the scientific view of the world" in an "educational system grounded in the humanistic and scientific traditions of the West" (Schlegel/Barry 1991:201). But such a glossed over view is undoubtedly countered by the innumerable examples of colonial education patterns, missionary schools, and the ensuing making of a "divided self"[14]; and generally, their assumptions about modern adolescence are rather speculative.

A different topic altogether lacking in Schlegel/Barry's analysis but an important aspect of adolescence, are data about the initiation into a society's main drug(s). These would be complementary to the authors' approach to adolescence as the social development towards gender roles.

The study *Adolescence* is still a rewarding source in the field of social and cultural anthropology. But it is clear that the cross-cultural analysis of pre-industrial societies does not, apart from a historical point of view, hold many clues for research in contemporary urban society. Puberty, adolescence, and youth in a city like present-day Vienna must be seen in a context of global urban society, and under conditions where clear demarcations of life periods are almost non-existent, as they have taken on a completely different and fragmented form.

---

14   … expression borrowed from David Laing's book title (1967). On the colonial self, see Walter Mignolo (2000). See also Stuart Hall's autobiographical contribution *The Formation of a Diasporic Intellectual*, pts. I – III, in Wambu (1999).

b. The Study of Youth in Cities

I will now approach the study of youth in cities through a picture of Chicago, the "Windy City", from the first decades of the 20th century. I will discuss the ethnography carried out in this quickly growing industrial metropolis by Frederic Thrasher, scholar of the Sociology Department of the University of Chicago, and Albert Cohen's further considerations about working-class youth. Chicago, the city in the heart of the United States of America, was subjected to rapid economic and social expansion due to industrialization and immigration, and also became home to the urban rhythm and blues music, parent of most present-day black popular music.

The Windy City and the Chicago School of Sociology

The University of Chicago's Sociology Department, founded in 1892 by Albion Small, achieved international reputation from 1914 under Robert Park; he was a close friend of Booker Taliaferro Washington. Together, they investigated e.g. the condition of southern black farmers (Yu 2001:38), who were denied access to political participation and kept in dependency.

Chicago was rapidly growing, attracting workers from rural areas and Irish, Polish, Italian, and other European immigrants seeking jobs in the industries and slaughterhouses of the Windy City. Large groups of black people were moving up from the Deep South along the Mississippi, many blues musicians among them. The experiences of the dreadful decades of slavery echoed in the one-, two-, and three-lined repetitive and rhythmic blues songs. "Probably most important, the slaves ... emphasized rhythm over harmony. In a single song, they clapped, danced, and slapped their bodies in several different rhythms" (Szatmary 1991:2).

Blues, after its way up "Ol' Man River" to Chicago, turned into the electrified rhythm and blues, a fully-fledged urban music which addressed the new urbanites' troubles and concerns. They had earlier been more affected by rural scourges, as the blues song from 1903 tells:

Boll weevil, where you been so long?
Boll weevil, where you been so long?
You stole my cotton, now you
Want my corn.

The boll weevil, a worm that feeds on the cotton ball, also "ravaged the Mississippi Delta cornfields in 1915 and 1916" resulting in a large-scale exodus of black people from the rural South to the cities of the North. From 1910 to 1930, Chicago's black population swelled from 40,000 to 234,000. "It wasn't peaches and cream, man", as pianist Eddie Boyd told; but he and many others had hoped for less drastic racism and more jobs than in the South. Steel mills and the food-processing industries took on many workers, also due to the war and lower numbers of people immigrating from Europe (Szatmary 1991:3). Soon, the city of Chicago swelled with people from diverse backgrounds.

These circumstances turned the Chicago of the 1920s into one of the most quickly developing cities in the world, featuring a meat industry which used slaughtering methods that were copied for the Ford car assembly-line production (Giedion 1987:140f., Dany 2007:16). Chicago was "urban" in every way possible, industrializing with all the good and bad consequences connected to that process. Concurrently ran the strange, religion-inspired phenomenon of alcohol Prohibition.

And sociology, a new science in the USA, found itself amidst a booming urban landscape. Chicago was the perfect laboratory for the urban social scientists who found their way to Robert Park and his approaches and interests, and were eager to study the human being and his/her reactions to ever-changing, quickly-developing urban surroundings.

The researchers wished to better the living conditions of the poor and believed that ethnographic research was the best method for finding ways to improve people's lives. Due to the "commitment of the newly-founded university to the solution of contingent social problems" (Tomasi 1999:1), research should be immediately transformed into social action. For this goal, information was needed from the inside – the "emic" view from the perspective of the urban poor themselves. Thus the research methods of the Chicago social scientists were as close to the people as possible. The researchers also understood that financial help provided to the poor by the city or the state would not be able to reach target groups if they, the sociologists, failed to provide an accurate picture of the people and their needs (*Encyclopedia of Social Theory* 2006; Tomasi 1999).

It was in this spirit that the Chicago School of Sociology did some of the most spectacular and – in terms of research settings, methods, and scientific and human engagement – most fulfilling works of ethnography. Many of their studies have become classics. Books like H. W. Zorbaugh's *Gold Coast and the Slum* (1929), *Street Corner Society* by William Foote Whyte (1943), *Outsiders* by Howard Becker (1963) and the works of Nels Anderson (*The Hobo: The Sociol-*

ogy of the Homeless Man, 1923) and, later, Elijah Anderson (*A Place on the Corner,* 1978/2003, and *Streetwise,* 1990) have given us major clues into urban and youth anthropology. Robert Park and Ernest Burgess co-edited *The City* (nicknamed "the Green Bible", 1925), a reader on urban problems and settings in an industrialized capitalist world. Robert Redfield became a pillar of urban anthropology. Further important scientific approaches were elaborated by Erving Goffman (symbolic interactionism), and Peter Bogardus (scale of social distance).

The Chicago School of Sociology was firmly rooted in the thinking of Ferdinand Tönnies and Georg Simmel (Cahnmann 1981; Levine et al. 1981) with the view of cities and the presumably anonymous metropolis as *Gesellschaft,* opposed to rural *Gemeinschaft.* Robert Redfield established urban anthropology along the lines of this dichotomy.

The first study of youth in an industrial city, Chicago itself, was *The Gang: A Study of 1.313 gangs in Chicago* by F. Thrasher, which was published one year earlier than Margaret Mead's study from the South Seas.

Frederic Thrasher: The Gang

One cannot help but be impressed by the sheer number of gangs observed by Frederic Thrasher and, after many years of research, described in his 1927 book. Thrasher, acutely aware of the great danger that gang members would turn into large numbers of citizens with no sense of involvement in, or loyalty to, US American society as a whole, "urged keeping channels of communication open between adults and adolescents", as James F. Short, Jr. states in his Introduction to the 1963 edition of *The Gang* (p. xl).

In Thrasher's view, how do gangs form? Special conditions are necessary to turn perfectly "natural" forms of friendships, the "spontaneous play-groups … gangs in embryo" (Thrasher 1963:23) into true gangs. Thrasher found one of these conditions to be the lack of understanding the parents, who often came from rural Europe[15], had for their children's special circumstances and problems: "Their children on the streets of Chicago come into contact with a motley collection of diverse customs on the one hand and new situations on the other. Hence, they have needs of which their parents never heard" (Thrasher 1963:179). Moreover, the children's experiences with life in the US were almost always negative, resulting in a sense of alienation from, and hostility toward, it:

---

15 Thrasher does not tell us whether or not the parents' inability to understand their children's needs was an exclusively European immigrant problem, or extended to parents from rural or urban US American backgrounds as well.

Contacts with Americans are usually superficial and disheartening and for the child are limited to certain official contact with school teachers, employers, or police. ... Hence, the children of the foreign born do not come into contact with the best in American life, but, when they escape parental control and follow their own impulses, become Americanized only with reference to our vices (Thrasher 1963:180f.).

Gangs are different universes of discourse, using "little languages" of their own, with jokes, catchwords and songs that preserve the gang's past experiences (Thrasher 1963:190). Thus the boys were easily seduced by the feeling of free life a gang would give:

Once a boy has tasted the thrilling street life of the gang, he finds the programs of constructive agencies insipid and unsatisfying. Gradually the gang usurps time usually given to school and work, and, by supplanting home, school, church, and vocation, becomes the primary interest of the boy (Thrasher 1963:65f.).

This is partly a result of, and partly the cause for, the boys' alienation from wider society:

Almost everything – history, geography, art, music, and government – that is the common knowledge of the schoolboy of the middle classes, is entirely beyond the ken and experience of the gang boy. He moves only in his own universe and other regions are clothed in nebulous mystery. He is only vaguely aware of them, for they rarely cut his plane. ... He knows little of the outside world except its exteriors. He views it usually as a collection of influences that would suppress him and curtail his activities with laws and police, cells and bars. In one way or another he is denied effective access to the larger cultural heritages of the dominant social order (Thrasher 1963:181).

While it is quite logical that boys (girls to a much lesser degree) would prefer the attractions of gang life to the demands of school and a bland and sometimes harsh home life, Thrasher points out that the "larger community of gangland is no better able to provide for the boy than is the immigrant family" (1963:179). He is very clear about what is needed in society and lacking in the gangs, and indeed throughout the nation, namely intergroup morality:

The good citizen of today must possess something more than gang morality. He must live in a society where tolerance of other groups, responsibility toward them, and co-operation with them are essential to social order and general prosperity. To this end there is a need for intergroup morality. .... So it is that the politician, the grafter, the racialist, the religious fanatic, the chauvinist, the imperialist, and so on, are the higher exponents of gang morality: they are all Greeks and the barbarians must suffer (Thrasher 1963:212f.).

Thrasher's statement clarifies that he sees "the gang" not as a phenomenon of the immigrants and so-called lower classes, but as a defining and destructive force in US American society, which must be countered by a humanitarian approach of solidarity.

There are several themes of special importance in Thrasher's book which are relevant for my own adolescence study: group structures; the boys' rapid accommodation to the independent group life; and the dire need to keep the channels of communication open between the boys and society at-large. Other problems are the youth's limited knowledge generally and about other population groups in the city who exclude them, and the gangs' "closed group" outlook on life.

Albert Cohen: Delinquent Boys

Albert Cohen, sociologist and criminologist trained by T. Parsons in Harvard, takes a more theoretical view on gangs, and therefore his work is complementary to Thrasher's. Cohen investigates young male delinquency from an analytical and psychological perspective. Even though delinquency is not a major aspect of Viennese park youth, Cohen's ideas about the boys' exclusion from mainstream society, and their groups' reaction to these structures of exclusion, are relevant to my study.

Cohen argues that delinquent boys form their groups in response to the overwhelming middle class values of US America, which are based upon Protestant ethics (Cohen 1967:87ff.)[16]. The working-class boys, who inevitably share many of those values, despair at ever being able to fulfil these demands in conduct and at school. As a response, they turn those values upside-down;

---

16 From the 1950s onwards, the dominant way of life that has been established in the USA suburbs and mainstreamed via radio, television, movies, and advertisement, was "suburban middle class materialism". Suburban ethics were consumption-oriented and *not* religious. I thank Craig Crossen for this information. A vivid description of such suburban lifestyles is given Brian de Palma's movie *Carrie* (1976). Generally, the US horror genre loves to exploit these surroundings.

Cohen describes non-utilitarian, malicious, and negativistic acts of collective youth delinquency (Cohen 1967:25), and short-run hedonism (1967:30). These anti-individualistic property acquisition and anti-rational consumption are ways of feeling good with being bad. Most important is the "emphasis on group autonomy, or intolerance of restraint except from the informal pressures within the group itself" (Cohen 1967:31).

Cohen, in his concluding chapter "A Delinquent Solution", argues that, for a working-class boy, the

> *primary* problem of adjustment is in the area of ego-involved status differences in a status system defined by the norms of respectable middle-class society. The delinquent subculture of the working class boy has the primary functions: first, of establishing a set of status criteria in terms of which the boy can more easily succeed; and second, of enabling him to retaliate against the norms at whose impact his ego has suffered, by defining merit in terms of the opposite of those norms and by sanctioning aggression against them and those who exemplify and apply them (Cohen 1967:168, italics in original).

Cohen explains gang formation psychologically, deriving it from the boys' frustration over their inability to meet the demands of the dominant social order. The most important feature is the emphasis on group life, and while their group-based solutions (or subcultures[17]) are counter-dependent in that they turn the dominant values into their contraries, these are also creative and funny. In his emphasis on the delinquent boys' joint activities and togetherness, Cohen implicitly uses Tönnies' notions of *Gemeinschaft* and *Gesellschaft,* which were – together with Simmel's works – key for the Chicago sociologists. Youth groupings are adolescents' definite insistence on togetherness, running contrary to the anonymous metropolitan ways:

> We see, for the most part, gangs of boys *doing things together*: sitting on curbs, standing on the corner, going to the movies, playing ball, smashing windows and "goin' robbin'". … They are joint activities, deriving their meaning and flavor from the fact of togetherness and governed by a set of common understandings, common sentiments, and common loyalties (Cohen 1967:178, italics in original).

---

17   For a discussion of subculture concepts see Gelder (2005).

Not definitely mentioned by Cohen is the economic saturation, which forms the basis of middle-class values. Reaching this material saturation requires long-term planning over several generations, including the deferred gratification patterns of a prolonged education – not exactly something that economically strained population groups can afford.

In summary, the main stimuli for gang formation seen by Thrasher and Cohen are: the lack of understanding of their children's urban situation by parents of rural (European) backgrounds; the kids' exclusion from mainstream institutions and their consequent frustration due to their inculcation with their values; and the emphasis on group autonomy and group activities, which tend to result in a parochial outlook.

Aspects on Gangs and the City: Aidan Southall

As an up-to-date complement to Thrasher's and Cohen's works, I consult Aidan Southall and his view of gangs as youth-specific formations in the global metropolis. "Young male groups have been called gangs throughout American history", says Southall (thus placing the very concept of gangs into a US American context), "always linked to anxieties about violence". US gang history includes brutal New York "adult gangs up to 1,000 strong", and "murderous, drug-maddened Black youth gangs of today's ghetto", next to which the "youth gangs of the 1930s and 1950s seem tame and almost respectable" (2000:393f.). After considering the role of schools – "Bad schools lead to truancy, delinquency, violence, unemployment and drug addiction, knitting together many urban scourges" – he closes with the dry statement that "gangs decrease with employment" (Southall 2000:395).

Southall sees youth gangs, such as the US American variety, as urban social phenomena linked to cities and metropolises in turbo-capitalist conditions. Gang processes are quite independent of ethnic backgrounds, follow social dynamics, and Southall perceives the function of youth gangs as "organizing otherwise lost and abandoned, anomic youth" (Southall 2000:393f.).

In urban settings, determined by the variety of human relationships and people's concentration, youth groups are the specific formations through which young people explore and experience their city surroundings, and then reflect upon and internalise them, influencing and being influenced by city lifestyles. Under social conditions of poverty, unemployment and precarity, gang processes will ensue from already formed groups, and a gang organizes economic resources for their members, thus filling in the gap between society at-large and the impoverished gang members', and often their families', needs and wishes.

Rather than perceiving adolescents merely as reacting against conditions they do not like, and as growing into something pre-determined, they often will creatively shape their surroundings and develop new approaches. Such practices are especially interesting in studies of immigrant youth in a former colonial power, Great Britain.

Youth in Great Britain

The Empire Windrush

The SS *Empire Windrush* was a huge steamer that brought the first large groups of Jamaicans to the shores of the imperial "Mother country" in 1948, with many more to follow (Sewell 1998; Phillips and Phillips 1999; Wambu 1999). The people aboard the ship had been recruited in Jamaica by official British agencies to work in the transport and health services in post-War London, which was suffering from severe war damage and a lack of working people. Immediately upon arrival the newcomers were struck by the fact that they saw white Britons doing hard work at the docks – a sight unknown to them in the Caribbean, where whites had merely run the country without doing any of the hard work (Sewell 1998:35; Phillips and Phillips 1999:45). Ashore, the new arrivals dispersed to several London districts, especially Notting Hill (mainly people from Trinidad and Tobago) and Brixton (mainly the Jamaicans), working-class areas with small Victorian houses where some Britons would rent to "blacks". Brixton's Coldharbour Lane, Railton Lane, and Atlantic Road – later dubbed "the Brixton Frontline"[18] – housed many immigrants, and Brixton is still today a predominantly Jamaican area[19]. Brixton has been, and still is, a focus of major unrest and skirmishes between the London police and the mostly black population, including many youths. The largest such riots took place from 10th to 12th April in 1981.

The 1998 Fiftieth Anniversary of the *Empire Windrush*'s landing prompted the publication of many books, both fiction and documentary. Particularly interesting is O. Wambu's 1999 volume *Empire Windrush. Fifty Years of Writing*

---

18 This name is widely used and appears e.g. as chapter heading in Rocky Carr's 1998 novel *brixton bwoy* where the author pictures Pupatee, an immigrant boy from Jamaica, and his coming of age in 1960s South London.

19 This chapter also refers to a short data collection in Jamaica and Brixton 1998 – 9. I am grateful to Sharon James, Mrs. "Auntie" Winnie Palmer, and to their relatives in Lucea and Kingston and in Great Britain, who accommodated me in 1998. Thanks also to Thorkild Gantner.

about Black Britain. Black British writers – including Stuart Hall, Paul Gilroy, Hanif Kureishi, Linton Kwesi Johnson, and Grace Nichols – came forth to speak about their experiences in England[20].

Great Britain and Youth "Between Cultures"

In 1977 James L. Watson published the edited volume *Between Two Cultures. Migrants and Minorities in Britain.* The authors (Nancy Foner, Verity Sayfullah Khan, Roger and Catherine Ballard, J. Watson himself, and others) present studies from both ends of the migration chain, including the effect of emigration on the migrants' home societies, mostly villages with subsistence and cash-crop farming. This bifocal approach to fieldwork is rewarding as it highlights the changing conditions in both the old and the new home, and the differing experiences that first-generation immigrants and their offspring face in the new country, with the new ways of life.

There are interesting data on youth in the volume, and it gets explained how especially the British-born "are caught between the cultural expectations of their parents (the first-generation migrants) and the social demands of the wider society. Young Sikhs and Jamaicans, for instance, often feel that they do not 'fit' in either culture" (Watson 1979:3).

For Sikh groups of rural South Asian origin, Roger and Catherine Ballard write, "For the second generation, however, the fact that they are not accepted – symbolised by the continued public categorisation of them as 'immigrants'– is crucial." While their parents had kept "the narrow loyalties of their homelands – based on caste and kinship", for young people it was urgent to react to unequal treatment (Ballard and Ballard 1979:54). This indicates an emerging solidarity among and between young people and youth groups who are discriminated against due to their "race".

One aspect of such solidarity is the black youth culture, which as a movement against racism, included reggae clubs and youth centers. Nancy Foner explains that the second generation adolescents of Jamaican descent, like their parents, "straddle two worlds" (Foner 1979:144), but have different and more frustrating life experiences, especially brought about by the deteriorating economic situation, and their ensuing vulnerability to unemployment. They are

---

20 Comparable to the *Empire Windrush* anniversary celebrations was the exhibition *Gastarbajteri* at the Wien Museum Karlsplatz, which celebrated 40 years of work migration to Austria. It took place in 2004 and included immigrants' personal archives and materials.

also more critical towards racism than their parents, as the adolescents are more perceptible of racial prejudice and discrimination (Foner 1979:145).

Among Pakistanis in Bradford, Verity Saifullah Khan observes how parents are worried about the multiple influences on their kids, especially their daughters, countering even the most orthodox home life, also via television (Khan 1979:85). Connected to an extended period of adolescence in Britain, "daughters and sons not only explore themselves but the various social worlds in which they participate" (Khan 1979:86). These processes are new to parents, and difficult for them to come to terms with.

James Watson says of the Chinese groups he worked with, that traditional attitudes were reinforced among the migrants in London, also by "the insecurities of work in an alien society", and that identification with their lineage was even stronger than among those who did not come abroad (Watson 1979:206). These processes connected to re-migration and the idealization of "back home" are therefore not promoting social and cultural change.

While Watson's volume is an implicit call for studying youth as a separate group in anthropological research, I find some relevant results for my research in these contributions from the 1970s pre-Thatcher era, such as the deteriorating job situation and the increasing importance of "back home" connections. Young people's experiences differ from their immigrant parents', and result in less tolerance of racism and a greater sense of alienation from the majority society, but also in growing solidarity with people in similar conditions.

During Great Britain's post-imperial 1970s, new groups formed around new musical styles. To illustrate adolescents and young adults creatively striving for new political structures, I will discuss Paul Gilroy, whose account of youth activism explicitly exposes their exclusion due to racism. Resistance movements and their impact on society can bring about far-reaching changes, and young people's participation in these is crucial, as Helena Wulff shows. Finally, Gerd Baumann's study on London's suburb of Southall will be explored regarding the inhabitants' interpretations of the terms "culture" and "community". These authors are relevant to my own work as they highlight the immigrants' active involvement in social and political change, and the specific ways in which young people do this.

There Ain't No Black ... Paul Gilroy and the Politics of "Race"

Gilroy was a scholar with the Birmingham Centre for Contemporary Cultural Studies. In his introduction to *There Ain't No Black in the Union Jack*[21], he criticizes Cultural Studies and their ethnocentric dimensions brought about by the "morbid celebration of England and Englishness from which blacks are systematically excluded" (Gilroy 2000:12).

In his book, originally published in 1987, Gilroy writes about youth in England from a political-activist position, and does not discuss them as static "cultural" groups[22]. Gilroy describes the post-racial stance of politically (re-)acting people, especially young Jamaicans, punks, and those associated with them, and the creative ways in which they took up these challenges: punk and reggae, and the expression in dystopian styles and visions[23].

Gilroy shows the influence that (British) Jamaicans had on the predominantly working-class punks and on their music, and the punks' outspoken anti-racist, anti-monarchist position, which was also critical of their own being white. Their political activism was centered in the Rock Against Racism movement.

Gilroy describes the punks' reaction to the Royal Silver Jubilee in 1977, which "brought festivities – street parties, school holidays – and an explosion of monarchist memorabilia which pushed the icons and symbols of a royalist and patriotic definition of Britishness and the British nation to the fore", linking white ethnicity, "race", and nationalism. The punks' "assault on the central icons of patrician British nationalism, particularly the Queen's face (transformed by safety pins[24] on the cover of the Sex Pistols' 'God Save The Queen'

---

21   The title refers to a National Front (the extremist British rightwing party) racist parole (Sewell 1998:3). Gilroy writes (2000:43ff.) about Powell's racist attacks and says, "that the new racism's newness can be gauged by its capacity to operate across the broad range of political opinion". Gilroy goes on, analysing Raymond Williams "as a striking example of the way in which the cultural dimensions of the new racism confound the left/right distinction" (Gilroy 2000:49).

22   In contrast to, for example, his colleague in Cultural Studies, Dick Hebdige, whose static view of the punk movement and semiotic efforts to grasp the "hidden" or "opaque" meaning of sub-cultural signs constrain his analytic abilities (*Subculture – The Meaning of Style*, 1991 [1979]). His merging of antagonistic youth sub-cultures is problematic and a-political, a culturalization of resistance and political movements, just like Diederichsen pointed out in his contribution "Wie aus Bewegungen Kulturen und aus Kulturen Communities werden", in: Fuchs, Moltmann and Prigge (1995).

23   Especially lucid are Poly Styrene's lyrics; she performed with her band, the X-Ray Spex, from 1976 on.

24   The artwork was by Jamie Reid; see Sladen, M. and Yedgar, A. (2007).

which was the number one record in Jubilee week), was an important symbolic manifestation … in their sub-culture". In that context, "a disavowal of white-ness was called for, not by the blacks themselves but by punk culture's own po-litical momentum". In ironic style, both neo-fascists' (explicitly) and popular nationalism's (implicitly) "mystic and metaphysical significance" of race was strictly rejected (Gilroy 2000:123f.).

Gilroy specifies concrete political actions and interventions while acknowl-edging the constant self-reflective interaction, communication, and transfer of ideas, work, and values among young people. He provides a description of a self-enacted youth movement, people who incorporated their experiences and commented and acted loudly and conspicuously against racial Britain, and for post-raciality.

Nancy Foner had hinted at that in her British-Jamaican study; and Helena Wulff's work shows how girls in the 1980s lived this vision in their styles and attitudes.

Helena Wulff, "Interracial Friendship in South London"

Wulff's contribution in the 1995 collection *Youth Cultures*, which she and V. Amit-Talai co-edited, is a review of her early 1980s fieldwork among girls in South Lon-don[25]. Wulff shows how the girls, as cultural agents, managed ethnic mixture, and insisted on their multiracial friendships and on their equality, "which is bound to have an increasing political impact in the long run" (Wulff 1995:77). Girls might be "often in the forefront of cultural mixture" (Wulff 1995:64).

The South London girls' experiences of racial equality and inter-racial friend-ship show a profound and self-established, self-determined resistance against racist practice, politics, and society[26]. Helena Wulff's idea that girls are "cultural agents in their everyday lives" holds a broader meaning: these girls are the fore-runners of a post-racial Britain which cannot exclude the immigrant minorities' impact and criticism and their relevant share in transforming the former British Empire. Wulff's contribution brings the political agency of young girls into focus and shows how change and progress also come from adolescents' changed out-looks and from incorporated experiences: bodily sensations instigated through consumption and expression of youth styles and music.

---

25 Wulff, Helena, *Twenty Girls* (1988).
26 Perhaps even more so in the wake of the Brixton riots in 1981, brutally suppressed by a po-lice force gone mad. The Brixton riots are not explicitly mentioned in Wulff's contribution, but surely were a major defining political experience of young (black) people at that time.

Gerd Baumann: Contesting Culture

An in-depth study of the mid-1990s is Gerd Baumann's *Contesting Culture* (1996). Baumann seeks for the meanings people give to such terms as *culture* and *community*[27] in Southall population groups. Baumann examines group formation processes among the residents of Southall, a suburban borough west of London. In discussing the respondents' uses of the terms *culture*, *community* and *ethnicity*, Baumann finds that two discourses exist, which he calls "demiotic" and "dominant". The latter "equates ethnic categories with social groups under the name 'community', and it identifies each community with a reified culture" (Baumann 1996:188ff. For a discussion of these terms see also Diederichsen 1995).

In the demiotic discourse, on the other hand, Southallians create new communities as well as subdivide or fuse existing ones. Culture and community are separated in the demiotic discourse, and their meanings reconsidered. But the demiotic discourse, Baumann insists, "is not an autonomous opposite, or independent alternative, to the dominant one. It is used to undermine the dominant one whenever Southallians ... judge it useful", while the dominant discourse is, for "so-called immigrants and ethnic minorities ... the currency within which they must deal with the political and media establishments on both the national and the local level." It "represents the hegemonic language within which Southallians must explain themselves and legitimate their claims" (Baumann 1996:192f.).

In course of his research, Baumann asked children to write short answers to *culture*-related questions, and he found Southallian children to share a collective *Kulturbewusstsein*: the "heightened awareness that one's own life, as well as the lives of all others, are decisively shaped by *culture* as a reified heritage" (Baumann 1996:98). This Kulturbewusstsein mirrors Great Britain's then current and dominant discussions of culture as a "self-evident" objective of communities. This consciousness of culture and community changes when children come of age: "juveniles often discover that in a variety of contexts they perform a youth culture of peers, as distinct from the cultures of their elders," and he shows how adolescents come to construct e.g. an *Asian* culture, a much wider reference than their parents' (Baumann 1996:146ff.), which reminds of the Ballards' findings in the 1970s.

Baumann brought to attention how the dominant discourse, including legal and political structures, strongly influences and determines young urban

---

27   All contested terms in Baumann's book are in italics.

adolescents' lives. Kulturbewusstsein also means awareness of discrimination on the grounds of an ascribed "cultural belonging". Being addressed and represented as "ethnic minorities", as belonging to "communities" (as *Ausländer, Neo-Österreicher, Muslime, Türken,* 2nd or 3rd generation) with "their different cultures" will yield reactions to such representations, as the park youth groups' ethnography will show.

c. Selected Current Research Approaches

Youth Studies at the Institute for Social and Cultural Anthropology, Vienna

There are several anthropologists in Vienna who have already contributed to the study of youth[28].

Anna Streissler focussed on youth studies both in her diploma work and in her dissertation. In Bogotá and Mexico City she concentrated on middle-class youth because she believed that these groups have been neglected in research, scientific interest in Latin American studies being biased towards deprived groups (Streissler 1997, 2003). Martin Slama worked on internet use and chatting in Indonesia, which also involves mainly middle-class youth and students, who thereby gained spheres both on- and off-line for their leisure activities and romance (Slama 2003, 2010).

Work on young Viennese with migration backgrounds was carried out by Dilek, Gürses, Herzog-Punzenberger, Reiser, and Strasser (1999). The authors, using group interviews, applied an anti-essentialist point of view and arrived at important conclusions concerning identity-forming processes. Adolescents' affiliation with parks and park groups, however, are not explored.

Adelheid Pichler, in her *Girls go guuurrrl* (2000), provides, in the context of analysing notions of girls' cultures, a study of female adolescents' biographies, and discloses the gender-connected status barriers in the job and labor markets. Her analysis is ethnographically based on feminist social and casework. In a similar vein, Daniela Digruber researched young women of the second generation after labor migration and asked about their work situations (2003), and points out how their proneness to giving up easily and perceiving themselves as "lazy" results from their frustration at their general lack of information, opportunities, and support.

---

28   See also Binder, Seiser, Streissler (2004).

HipHop Grows! Graffiti Einsiedlerpark

Susanne Binder, expert on intercultural education, researched interaction in multicultural schools and classrooms, processes of inclusion/exclusion, identity forming, and negotiations in growing up (2004).

Recent work in social and cultural anthropology has been done by Sonja Siegert who studied children's park groups during her professional work in leisure-time activity training in the 15th District. She provides marvellous insights into the groups' structures and their mutual recognition (2009).

Approaches from Other Disciplines

There are quite a few academic works by researchers from other disciplines who have also worked in Vienna with similar, and partially the same, groups as myself.

An extensive and most enlightening study from the 1990s comes from psychologist Gudrun Schuster. She researched intercultural communication in her work with schoolgirls in Vienna's Brigittenau (1994). Schuster develops her analysis from dyadic interviews and arrives at very detailed results concerning mutual ascriptions, prejudices, demarcations, and opinions.

Susanne Deimel-Engler worked on Turkish adolescent girls' educational situation (1997), and Sonja Gruber (2000) has done sociological research on

Turkish Muslim park boys in the 5th District. Gruber attempts to explain how the adolescents' cultural backgrounds influence their attitudes and behavior. Gruber also researched girls' park uses (1999, 2002).

Youth sociologist Natalia Wächter studied young migrant adolescents' chat room interactions (2004), and analysed *Jugendkultur in Wien* in a historical perspective (2006). Annelies Larcher did her qualitative research on adolescent girls (2007) in the context of women's studies in sociology. She shows how girls, under-represented in parks and football cages, actively shape their leisure time together and often stray out of the district, following their interests in meeting people as they escape control.

For his medical degree, Benjamin Schindlauer researched park adolescents' attitudes towards health. He concluded that increased medical attention to park-based kids is essential because of the health risks from their surroundings, their living circumstances, and their own health behavior (2008).

Numerous studies come from ethnographic diploma works of social and youth workers. These contributions share a precise understanding of young people's lives, and are guided by partiality and advocacy.

The study of adolescents generally benefits from an interdisciplinary approach, and relevant research comes from several directions. However, in order to study park youth groups, it is also necessary to look into work on urban space, and into concepts of groups.

4. Urban Space and Urban Landscape

The city as social space, in which social interaction came to be "mediated more and more by money", is dominated by commerce. Cities and metropoles are sites of mass consumption, marked by "struggles over access to public space and public display in the face of privatized capital interests". City architecture, street construction, policing and municipal social control are mediated expressions of (state) power ("Urbanism and Urbanization", *Encyclopedia of Social Theory*, 2006).

Anthropologists turned to urban space especially in urban anthropology. E. Eames and J. Goode, in their *Introduction to Urban Anthropology* (1977), spoke e.g. of parks and other leisure-time areas to be researched as "units of integration" (1977:225f.). For example, Martha Wolfenstein focussed on children in metropolitan parks in Paris, and compared them, their play, and their upbringing to those in the US (1955).

Anthropologists who chose to study urban spaces in particular are Setha Low, Kathrin Wildner, and Theodore Bestor. Low worked *On the Plaza* in Costa Rica (2000); Wildner analysed the *Zócalo*, the huge square forming Mexico City's center (2003); and Ted Bestor studied *Tsukiji*, the Tokyo Fish Market (2004).

Coming to approaches to Vienna, urban anthropologist Robert Rotenberg researched gardens (1995). He analyses the historical development of the Vienna city landscape (1995:23ff.) and, basing his work on Foucault's idea of *heterotopia* (extraordinary places, absolutely different), Rotenberg finds that people's images and ideas of urban landscape mirror their concept of society: urban landscapes are ideology-based models of community life. The neighborhood parks of my study would be then, in Rotenberg's model, residual, marginal urban space, which becomes symbolically identified with the park users and their position in Viennese society.

Urban surroundings and their divisions are, according to urban geographers P. Marcuse and R. van Kempen, the "spatial translation" of macro-social forces, macro-economic processes, and social dividing lines between population groups (Marcuse/van Kempen 2000:20). These spatial socio-economic divisions are not very strongly expressed in Vienna. The districts I call "old working-class" are generally not run-down or neglected, and their inhabitants are people with a variety of lifestyles, including students, and artists.

Jane Jacobs, critical observer of urban renewal policies, and grassroots activist promoting creative and workable cities, describes how urban dwellers can live a mutual responsibility for each other without necessarily knowing each other, an intersubjective and intergroup solidarity. It is thus, and in such public spaces, that children and then adolescents with their different uses and also different desires and needs, can grow up, learning the responsible ways of the city. A prerogative for that is, in Jacob's view, urban architecture and city planning: with variable spaces, a multiple user profile, and a petty capitalist economic structure (ice cream parlors, tobacco shops, groceries). Neighborhood is the supporting social concept in which relationships and solidarity ground and grow on. This enables safe playing surroundings for children, who must be given enough room for their development efforts. All these structures, thriving on well-working neighborhood diversity, lead to a street feeling which counters anonymity, and enable quick communicative support among people. Children get to know, and to trust adults (Jacobs 1993:97 ff.).

With coming of age, children's priorities and activities change. As they grow into adolescence, this process should be integrated into city life as well:

> As children get older, this incidental outdoor activity – say, while waiting to be called to eat – becomes less bumptious physically and entails more loitering with others, sizing people up, flirting, talking, pushing, shoving and horseplay. Adolescents are always being criticized for this kind of loitering, but they can hardly grow up without it. The trouble comes when it is done not within society, but as a form of outlaw life (Jacobs 1993:113).

Jacobs strictly rejects confining those coming of age away to special grounds, which is often propagated as solution for adolescents in densely populated urban space. Viennese neighborhood parks, the spatial units of this book, could be taken to be such special zones for children and adolescents, but parks are integral parts of their neighborhoods as well.

Public neighborhood parks in Vienna are certainly largely uncontrolled, not commercialized, and open, and therefore could be taken as "spaces of escape", which Ash Amin and Nigel Thrift describe (Amin/Thrift 2002:119). However, the urban geographers are realistic: "Most such spaces are only brief respites ... And some of those spaces are either generally dangerous or they are dangerous to particular groups of the population" (Amin/Thrift 2002:123f.).

Shopping high street: Mariahilfer Strasse

Researching such neighborhood parks from the standpoint of urban land-scape design, Laura Jeschke's study (2000) shows how the weaker and less mobile groups are hindered in their appropriation of park space. Those in need of leisure time space in their living quarters are people who are less mobile: older people, children, and adolescents. Access to public space is, like the availability of other material and immaterial goods, dependent on social status (Jeschke 2000:71), and to seize, to make accessible, and to shape such space can be difficult for weaker groups such as senior citizens and younger girls. These, especially from 10 to 13 years of age, are often powerless in the parks (Jeschke 2000:77). It is therefore necessary to involve urban planning in favor of such groups to enhance their chances to appropriate urban public space in their neighborhoods.

I am not studying parks as such, but try to describe the adolescents who use parks as their main social focus. Encompassing all the above, and in order to approach adolescents' use of parks, I have chosen Victor Turner's concept of an "arena", as the symbolic yet actual place of conflict.

The Arena: Victor Turner's Concept

Victor Witter Turner's work and theories, derived from ample fieldwork and his broad-minded interest in various areas, provide a good vantage point from which to perceive adolescence and the urban youth in this study. Turner was influenced crucially by Margaret Mead's *Coming of Age in Samoa* and, later, by Arnold van Gennep's *Les rites de passage* (Petermann 1989, Schomburg-Scherff 2001). He did not concern himself with youth studies, but developed his interest in transitory rituals in his fieldwork with the Ndembu (in what is today Zambia). In his essay "Betwixt and Between: The Liminal Period in Rites de Passage" (1963; published in *The Forest of Symbols*, 1967), Turner presents his concept of liminality – the middle, separated, or "de-linked" stage of such rites.

Turner elaborated his idea of liminality into a much broader concept, which he applied to diverse manifestations of human society, and which is contextual for him with freedom, new ideas, and creativity. He operated with the dichotomy of *communitas* and *structure* (or *societas*), which remind us of *Gemeinschaft* and *Gesellschaft* as Ferdinand Tönnies used them.

"Arena" is a term from political anthropology recurrently used by Victor Turner and others (e.g. Swartz, Turner, and Tuden 1976). For Turner, arenas are the "concrete settings in which paradigms become transformed into metaphors and symbols with reference to which political power is mobilized and in which there is a trial of strength" (1994:17), "a scene for the making of a

Einsiedler Park with graffiti wall, Wien – Margareten

Breakers-to-be

decision" (1994:135). Social dramas are played out in these arenas, which are also marked by symbolism and style (Turner 1994:133ff.), whereas political fields "are the abstract cultural domains where paradigms are formulated, established, and come into conflict", for example over exclusion rules (1994:17).

In this study, the term "arena" is used for the parks as the most important meeting places for the park adolescent groups. Parks constitute an arena: contested places, where interactions and decisions define the park youths' experiences, activities, and views, while the entire city, as Aidan Southall maintained, is also the arena for the "fateful drama" of humankind.

To conclude, Viennese neighborhood parks are non-commercialized, devalued arenas for excluded groups who symbolically and practically act out their view of themselves in society. Parks are *heterotope* spaces, dependent and perceived as marginalized. Commercialization of space has not reached the parks, however, so that they manifest liminality as well; this is a counter-argument vis-à-vis the assumption of a complete interspersing of urban space with money-based relations. But parks are also contested spaces of escape and arenas for multiple asymmetric appropriations, where sometimes, weaker groups are pushed aside.

But spatial contexts of park adolescents in Vienna also comprise spaces that are not public, or not material. The former are shopping malls: urban models in protected, closed containers in which experiences of the city are put on stage (Hoffmann-Axthelm 1995:66); and the latter are virtual spaces, of increasing importance for social relations and economic transactions where (urban) space and place are ever less important, and new forms of "technosociality" come into being. These contexts will be considered later in the ethnography.

5. Groups

All adolescents in the public parks and cages of Vienna's working-class districts are part of a peer group. As institutions like the family become less important, or less adequate, for the young person, their emotional need for a peer group (*clique*) rises. Cliques that lack resources are especially dependent on public space, as they cannot afford to meet elsewhere.

Peer Group and Network Concepts

The term "peer group", introduced to US American youth sociology by C.H. Cooley, describes "informelle Spiel- und Freizeitgruppen von etwa gleichaltrigen Kindern und Jugendlichen" (informal play- and leisure-time groups of children and adolescents who are roughly of the same age). The peer group is a *Sozialisationsinstanz* and helps young people to initiate social separation and orientation processes, and to cross the emotional barriers which were formed in childhood. New social experiences are made in the groups (Hillmann 2007). Youth sociologist Klaus Hurrelmann states in his *Einführung in die Sozialisationstheorie*, that peer groups connect the family with the political, economic, and cultural realms of society, as the peer group's (and also the mass media's) influence becomes stronger than the family's (Hurrelmann 2006:239f.).

Anthropological approaches to adolescent peer groups are scarce. Schlegel and Barry collect material on them: in their view, the function of such groups is the prevention of in-breeding, adolescent groups being the manifestations of exogamy.

In my ethnography I will simply use the term "groups", returning to a concept previous to "network". Groups, as J. Fuhse says in the *Encyclopedia of Social Theory*, imply a "boundedness, connectedness, and homogeneity"; rare on the empirical level, "the network concept increasingly displaced the group concept" (2006).

But for youth research, such a definition of group is accurate for the park peer groups I encountered. Further terms used here are "crowd": "adolescence marks the emergence of larger groups of peers, or crowds" (*The Gale Encyclopedia of Childhood and Adolescence*, 1998) and "scene", which are important for the broader context of urban adolescents and young adults in Vienna (and, via mass media and virtual connections, throughout the world), and imply a linkage, a sharing of styles and values, without necessarily being an intimate, personal relationship.

Check den Einsiedlerpark!

II. "We're Doing It in the Park!"

Ethnography of Park Youth in Vienna

1. The Arena

a. Vienna as an Urban Setting

The City of Vienna

Vienna is the venue of this study. It is a historical city, both as a former imperial capital and as an early bastion of the international labor movement. It is the capital of Austria but not a true metropolis. Its oldest core part is the Roman settlement Vindobona, and Vienna has grown in concentric circles around the grand medieval Stephansdom. Socio-economic factors divide the urban space into working-class, bourgeois, and elite areas, but without slums, ghettos, and no-go areas: the municipality of Vienna has deliberately mixed population strata, with social housing in richer areas, and more affluent buildings of flats in working-class neighborhoods. There are no outright problem areas; single problem buildings are scattered throughout the city, with a certain concentration of such houses in the poorer districts.

Vienna is integrated in globalization processes and touched by them in various ways. These processes include migration and refugee movements, the social and cultural impact of global marketing strategies, and various processes of socio-economic transformation.

Austria was not one of Europe's strong colonial powers with transatlantic, African and Asian colonies, but of great inner-European dominance especially in South and South-East Europe. A small middle European country now, with a long-standing history of labor migration and with new arrivals (refugees, labor migrants, students), Austrian society becomes increasingly diverse and multi-lingual.

Urban Experiences of Exclusion, Post-Raciality, and Neo-Nationalism

Roughly four-fifths of the park adolescents are from working-class immigrant or refugee backgrounds and have grown up bilingually (*Jahresbericht Back On Stage 5*, 2006). They are therefore personally caught up in the transnational global economic processes about which Gingrich and Banks, Sassen, and Ivekovic speak. Many of the labor-dependent youths in Vienna are involved in the immigrant experience of their parents or other relatives, or of friends and acquaintances, and share a heightened awareness of negative ascriptions – a Kulturbewusstsein in Baumann's sense.

First of all, these kids share experiences of diverse forms of racism connected with language, hair, skin and eye color, name, and other ethnic markers, which often result in exclusion, harassment, bureaucratic troubles with visa and other documents, unjust treatment (both deliberate and unintentional), increased police surveillance, and a general denial of human rights. Park youth are, whether through own or friends' experience, well aware of such forms of discrimination[29].

In compulsory elementary education, many public schools (Volksschule, Hauptschule, Sonderpädagogische Zentren) have a very low proportion of pupils from monolingual German-speaking households. The reverse is true in private schools and the Gymnasium. Schools, especially those compulsory public schools with open access, are contested contexts; some discussions tend to "blame the victims" – especially the Kinder mit nichtdeutscher Muttersprache (children with a non-German mother tongue). They are sometimes held responsible for the bad schools, while actually they are the ones who most suffer from them. For that reason, middle-class families (with or without immigration backgrounds) increasingly enrol their kids in private schools, the more affordable of which are confessional.

There is a significant interdependence between district (poorer working-class areas with low rents) and percentage of working-class people with (former) alien citizenship. Older population sections are still predominantly native Austrian, but proportionally larger groups of the younger generations share a non-Austrian background. This indicates that most of Vienna's working-class youth grow up in neighborhoods and schools characterized by multilinguality, diversity of national origin, and, unfortunately, the scourge of poverty. Certain schools, blocks, or neighborhoods are in especially difficult circumstances.

Viennese adolescents who have grown up with others from diverse family backgrounds differentiate people by categories other than simple ethnic origin. These include categories of "open" and "closed" world-views. Many working-class adolescents long for post-racist and post-migrant, non-discriminatory surroundings, while others tend towards new concepts of ethnic stereotyping and neo-nationalism.

---

29 The artist Onur Serdar describes: "For example, in institutions, like when I give my visa application, I can see the same actions, these actions tell you: you are a foreigner, you are not with us, you are not from us" (Interview 2007).

Vienna from above: view from the Stephansdom

Vienna through Young People's Eyes

The relevant distinction in young people's perception of the city is that between the neighborhoods, and the common urban areas.

Neighborhoods

The working-class neighborhoods are interlaced with social relations and interactions, as a substantial part of the economic structure is based on family enterprises like groceries, bakeries, cheap-shops and supermarkets, local cafés, fast-food places, internet and mobile telephone shops, hairdressers and barbers. These small enterprises and local shops, and their owners and salespersons, are the catalysts in the districts, and young people are more or less acquainted with them or at least aware of them. The neighborhoods also comprise the schools, youth centers, and other social institutions important for the park youth.

Inner-city working-class districts of present-day Vienna resemble, in parts at least, Jane Jacobs' "ideal" New York neighborhoods as less anonymous urban space, in which the young urban city dwellers' lives are grounded.

View from the Belvedere

Reumannhof, Wien – Margareten

Common Urban Areas

The neighborhoods contrast with common urban areas interesting to young people. Youth from all over Vienna, and from all economic strata and backgrounds, frequent mainly the central Mariahilfer Strasse, with its international chain stores selling clothes, shoes, sportswear, multimedia and technology; and leisure time is spent in the recreational areas on the Donauinsel, the Copa Cagrana along the Danube, and the Prater.

A general trend of urban development is the capitalization of space, marked by the proliferation of open-air cafés, of "Schanigärten" (the open-air areas of the more traditional restaurants), of riverside clubbing and partying areas along the Danube and the Donaukanal, and of shopping malls. The urban common areas comprising the world of merchandising cater to what can be called young urban consumerism. A key feature in this consumer world is the array of shops and enterprises dedicated to the care and adornment of the body: hairdressers, manicurists, solariums, fitness studios and workout centers, and jewellery, piercing, and tattoo stores.

Neighborhood high street: Reinprechtsdorfer Strasse, Margareten

Schanigarten, Wien-Währing

Mariahilfer Strasse

These all are places where both sales people and customers are in many ways interrelated. Fast food restaurants, large department stores, supermarkets, and chain bakeries employ countless young, unskilled workers. Jobs in the low-paying service sector include vendors, guards and security personnel, ticket sellers, janitors, maintenance engineers, and sales clerks. At times the atmosphere in an establishment resembles that of a discotheque rather than that of a place of business. Friendship groups sometimes work in the same shop, which keeps at bay the loneliness and anonymity, which otherwise often makes wage labor quite a drag; and other friends drop by to visit them. This Vienna-wide youth-affine work and consumer world, established in the centrally located places which are frequented by all, spreads along the main shopping high streets in working-class areas which draw a more local crowd (Favoritenstrasse, Meidlinger Hauptstrasse), and peters out in smaller high streets and then towards the neighborhoods with their specific structures of locality. Focal points are also both centrally located, and working-class area shopping malls, which draw mixed crowds from a large zone of attraction.

b. Neighborhood Parks in Vienna

Beside the large and beautiful metropolitan parks (Volksgarten, Burggarten, Rathauspark, Stadtpark) around the elegant and imperial First District, and vast green areas such as the Prater, there are also the so-called *Beserlparks*[30] in the old working-class districts (2, 3, 5, 10, 11, parts of 12, 14 and 15, 16, 17, and 20). These districts are crowded and densely populated due to inexpensive old private housing with small and therefore cheap apartments, and there is a large proportion of social housing complexes, some of which – especially those from the inter-war period – are strikingly well-designed and speak of politicians', planners' and architects' devotion to good working-class living.

The neighborhood parks are not necessarily beautiful, but pragmatic, a sheer necessity in the densely populated poorer districts. The average park is perhaps 100 meters long and 70 meters wide, though there are some considerably larger and many smaller ones. Some neighborhood parks are square, surrounded by streets, others are hidden and remote. The parks share certain features, but each is unique in setting, layout, equipment and furnishings, age, size,

---

30 Term not translatable; a *Beserl* is a small broom. I call them "neighborhood parks", a term Jane Jacobs has used (1993:116 – 145).

and accessibility[31]. Typically they are equipped with a children's playground, some benches and tables, a water pipe (turned off in winter), litterbins, a "dog-zone", and sometimes a public toilet. And of course there are some trees and shrubs. Numerous small paved walks cross each park. A neighborhood park reflects, and depends on, the surrounding areas (Jacobs 1993:128).

Parks in these working-class neighborhoods are important spaces for people to meet and enjoy the open. Though often almost deserted during mid-day and in winter, on summer evenings a park will be crowded with people from the neighborhood passing their leisure hours outside.

Parks provide adolescents' groups with space for interaction, communication, and transfer in a unique way of life – the Viennese park life. I draw upon my long-term relationships, personal participation, observations, sharing of stories and collective experiences with park adolescents to describe how special aspects of youth – group formation, first experiences, music, processes of maturing and growing up, body practices – are lived out in parks and make up the park life.

Ball Play Cages

A central position in park life is held by the fenced-in courts, called "Käfige": the cages. Not every park has a cage, and there are cages in central metropolitan, and in upper- and middle-class area parks as well. Paved and fenced-in playgrounds, of which there are about 500 in Vienna, have been laid out in parks since the 1970s. The most prominent cages are those for soccer, and groups who have played in the cages have been many and diverse over the decades. Cages with larger space, higher fences, and better all-around layouts for soccer attract older and stronger users who tend to exclude younger and weaker groups[32].

Basketball was introduced to Vienna parks around the beginning of the 1990s. Superstars Michael Jordan and Magic Johnson impressed youth in Vienna via media and advertising, and by the middle of the 1990s, the basketball hype had resulted in the installation of metal baskets in many park cages. Bas-

---

31   Pictures and park descriptions on www.wien.gv.at/umwelt/parks.
32   For example, some well-designed cages, including a beach-ball cage, a basketball cage, and a nice soccer cage, are situated within the median of the Margaretengür-tel; these cages are only rarely used by the neighborhood adolescents, but by semi-organized groups of young grown-up males, and middle-aged men from the adjacent districts.

Bacherpark, Wien – Margareten

Ball Play Cage, Urban Loritz-Platz

ketball or streetball competitions accompanied by hiphop DJs, break dance, and graffiti actions were held in parks. Groups playing basketball made a point of being different from soccer players – more cosmopolitan, sophisticated, and suave. Basketball also takes less space, and streetball is played around one basket by both teams. However, the basketball craze seems to have waned among the youth, with the result that soccer has reclaimed its former dominance in the parks. Recently, the municipality, who thereby give notice to park groups' skills, arranges official park soccer competitions in cages each year, and there are also tournaments for girls.

Processes of exclusion, fission, and fusion occur around the cages. Established groups can co-exist, e.g. basketball groups and soccer groups and younger and older groups, though not necessarily on entirely friendly terms.

Contested Spaces of Escape

Cages are the most contested areas in the parks. Problems connected with parks and cages include complaints from the neighborhood and from bullied, blackmailed, or mugged children and teenagers about groups who lay exclusive claim to certain park areas and cages[33]. Park adolescents do in fact speak of "our park" and "our cage". But such notions can be – and often have been – very quickly dispelled by political decisions from the city. Several parks around the city have been targeted as sites for underground garages, which entails a major construction project that can severely curb a park's use for months. One of the parks designated for such construction was Bacherpark in the 5th District. But then some of the local residents took action:

> Bacherpark is squatted by the anti-garage movement who have had their tents on the designated building site since January 6th, 2006. The small resistance group has erected a press center over the children's sand box, a little hall of wooden poles and planks they built together with the park children. Inside, they cook meals, and prepare tea and coffee for everybody.

> The garage foes hold winter parties on Saturdays. The resident park and cage boys soon joined the resistance movement after initial mistrust. They understood that this is about their own interests: the park shall remain as it is, not be closed down for months to be "beautified". The kids were well

---

33   See also Blum/Kromer's chapter 'That's My Park!' Occupation of Territory, in Riepl and Williamson (2009:139ff.).

Sandbox, Bacherpark

Press center, Bacherpark

aware that they needed the park daily, and that, with the park closed, they would not be able to meet each other as regularly as they wanted to. Alternative meeting places and other cages to play soccer are not easy to find, and the adolescents realised that their groups would have shrunk or dispersed, would have been shattered.

The parks and cages are spaces contested not only by the occasional threat of subterranean garage construction, but by deteriorating park equipment, by police raids, and by conflicts with security personnel who lock the cages at night fall.

Dominance over, and oppression of, weaker and less powerful groups is sometimes played out in parks and cages by those situated at the margins and the bottom of society. Some cages are the last-ditch retreat zones for young men who cannot go anywhere else, and often they end up staying there for life. Individual and group violence against others in the parks is, in part at least, a reflection of society at-large. And Jane Jacobs stated that "the belief that uses of low status drive out uses of high status" is not consistent with "how cities behave ... People or uses with more money at their command ... can fairly easily supplant those ... of less status" (Jacobs 1993:127).

Apart from bullying, there are many other reasons why adolescents do not go to the parks in their neighborhood. But this study is about those who do, and it is time to see who comes to the parks, what types of groups they form, and how these groups interact. While all young people need to be with their peers, those who frequent the parks constitute a publicly visible set.

c. Who's in the Park?

At present, adolescent park life is an overall Viennese feature, to be experienced in parks in the old working-class districts, and, increasingly, in the many newly-built housing projects across the Danube and in Vienna's southernmost 23rd district.

The groups I have been acquainted with were quite distinct and some existed, in changing forms, over a decade or longer. The groups ranged in size from two or three persons up to twenty or more, with usually clear and exclusive affiliations: though individual members of different groups often knew each other, few participated in more than one group. But possibilities for interactions outside the group were many – school, the park, shopping high streets and malls, sports, youth centers. Thus the park kids were connected with numerous other groups and persons all over the district and in Vienna in varied ways, and this increased with a person's age and mobility.

Park adolescents are from diverse, often immigrant, backgrounds and families. Those who live near it, and have a social peer group already formed, frequent the parks. This is especially so for young boys, who often establish their park play groups while still rather small children and go to the park closest to their home; others stray further, where they eventually find peers to their liking.

Many of these parks are meeting places for numerous groups of adolescents, often throughout their youth. Each year, around 40 groups comprising approximately 300 adolescents made regular use of parks and cages in the comparably small 5th District, the largest portion of adolescent park users being boys between 14 and 16 years of age. The park adolescents' parents are, or were, citizens of Bosnia, Bulgaria, Albania, Croatia, Poland, Serbia, Macedonia – FYROM, Romania, Russia (Fed. Chechnya), Afghanistan, Turkey, Iraq, Great Britain, Chile, Vietnam, Sri Lanka, Nigeria, Morocco, and Somalia, as well as Austria itself. Park users also include Kurdish and Roma groups of various national and religious backgrounds (*Jahresbericht Back On Stage 5*, 2006). The present diversity of the park adolescents' parental national backgrounds contrasts with the results of our 1997 survey in which we found the 5th District's parks were used mainly by the offspring of the "classical" labor immigrants from Yugoslavia and Turkey (Mayer/Möderndorfer 1998).

Park adolescents cannot be understood as a mere and more or less accidental collection of migrant-background or marginalised youth. Not all of these adolescents frequent the park: many have never gained access to a group; others follow other interests; and still others, not wishing to become involved, stay at home. And not all adolescents in the parks are economically and socially marginalised.

Young people of majority background are there, either in or with groups, and there are middle-class kids and groups from more affluent social situations.

An answer to the question "Who is in the park?" must include a consideration of the proportion of male to female park users. A glance at any neighborhood park in Vienna's old working-class districts reveals a majority of boys – sometimes in some areas exclusively boys. This does not match what is seen in other urban public spaces (shopping high streets, subways, local streets), in which the sexes are about evenly distributed; nor what is observed in the large metropolitan parks which are also used by adolescents (Stadtpark, Burggarten); nor the demographics of leisure and recreation areas such as the Donauinsel, Donaupark, Prater, Steinhofgründe, and Kahlenberg, where families are the primary user groups. The parks we are considering must therefore have special features, which encourage boys to use them.

Boys and Girls in the Park

Girls make up around one-third of a district's adolescent users of public space – but not necessarily of the parks. The park-user structures of girls and boys differ, with girls tending to avoid the parks when they are older, or during colder weather and later hours[34].

Parks are especially used by boys to play soccer, a pastime also connected to future aspirations. Soccer can accommodate many players – the more the better – and is quite an absorbing game. The physical nature of the game, and the adverse playing conditions (rough asphalt pavements) are especially demanding. Such conditions do not encourage girls to take part in the game.

In addition to being the majority in sheer numbers, some boys are also strikingly open about their generally negative opinions concerning girls in the park. In 1999, during the re-structuring of Einsiedlerpark into a "geschlechtssensiblen" (gender-sensible) park, a 13-year-old boy was asked his opinion about girls' park use:

Q: Should girls have space in the park, too? – A: No! – Q: Why not? – A: Because they bother us! (Interview with Al., 1999.)

---

34   See also the new study *Expedition: Jugend-Zone. Sozialraumanalyse Wien – Ottakring*; adolescent researchers from the youth center were included to investigate their favorite hang-outs (the study is available on-line from www.jugendzentren.at).

This interview was conducted during the period after Einsiedlerpark's much-frequented soccer cage had been changed into a multi-functional ball play area, much to the frustration of the former cage's soccer groups. But many boys, like Al., consider the parks "their" spheres, and think that girls have neither the right, nor any good reason, to be there.

Girls in the Park

Ma. from Eremitpark, which is directly behind her house, is blond and slim, with a clean face and inquiring eyes. She is a basketball fanatic and comes to the park to play with her friends. Tupac Shakur is her idol, and every time we meet her she wants to know more about him. – This was when she was twelve. She stopped coming to the park soon after; others told us that she joined a real sports club, where she spends her leisure time now, playing basketball with a team. She was, when still attending the park, very much interested in the re-structuring of the park, and one of the most engaged in discussions about how the whole laying-out of the place, and the future ball cage, should be.

Ma. is a good example of a girl who found other, obviously better, leisure time facilities when she got older. She did not simply wish to hang around, but was quite focused on her sports activities, and the necessary resources were obviously provided by her family.

Sh.'s parents fled from Afghanistan many years ago, with intervening stays in Pakistan, India, and Czechoslovakia. She is from a large family, with six sisters and two brothers. Her friend Me. is native Viennese.

Sh. and her best friend Me. are 11 years old, and can be found almost daily on the edge of Wolkenkratzer Park where they play. They know a lot about the going-ons in the park, but keep their distance from other user groups. They also frequent other spaces: one time we meet them on a bench in a smaller side street; then in the Flusser Park, and in the Eremit Park. Both girls are friends from school, doing quite well there (2006).

Girls often form very strong relationships with one or two female friends. A special feature of girls' relationships is the almost twin-like bonding that can occur between two girls: they will be constantly together, share everything, and often wear identical, or each other's, clothes. For them, a dyadic tie with another girl on equal terms seems to be the most important social structure (see also Geisler 1996), and they are likely to meet with their best friend first, and then go to a park, or somewhere else with her.

Many girls have their own ways of using public space, ways that are not necessarily territorial, not centered on one specific park. They are demanding groups to establish contact with: they might be easily overlooked if one exclusively researches only one park in a neighborhood, or does not take into account the general public spaces of a neighborhood and the district. Girls are often in these areas to escape the control of parents and/or brothers and therefore are frequently wary of outsiders.

Girls will also sometimes drop by the park while running an errand, or on the way home from school, to see if their friends happen to be there (Mayer 1999). Girls shift between parks more often than the boys. They frequent the remoter areas of the parks, especially favoring the children's playgrounds with swings. They tend to sit quietly on the margins of the parks or in the playgrounds, are less active in sports, and are often in small groups of two or three. They want and need to know what's going on, who is there, "wo sind Buben" ("where are boys"), and where the "action" is, but observe from a remoter position. Girls will frequent a district's high streets in contrast to the boys, who often simply pass through on their way to a soccer ground. Girls also often go to main shopping streets like the cosmopolitan Mariahilfer Strasse, or the more working-class Favoritenstrasse in the 10th District. Girl groups, as Larcher (2007) observed, also use their time outside for long walks through the district and the city, especially to malls, shopping high streets, and the Donauinsel.

Girls tend to use the neighborhood parks of their childhood less as they get older. However, older girls might accompany their (new) boyfriend to his park to hang out with him and his group. This is especially so in "open" groups which, as their members grow up, venture out to common urban areas and clubs, and sometimes form large groups who will meet in their park as well.

In general, adolescent girls from well-off, middle-class entrepreneur families are strongly encouraged to go on to higher education and the university and are not frequently found in the parks. Study at the Gymnasium[35], for example, imposes a strict schedule, with classes in the afternoon, a large amount of homework, and often, extracurricular activities like music and sports, leaving

---

35 Austria's school system is based on early tracking: the Gymnasium is for 10 to 18 year old students, and provides a universalist humanist education. The final exams, the *Matura*, are a prerogative for the admission to universities.

little time for parks. The pupils might also be less interested in contact with park groups, which they might find boring and rough.

Girls who take the veil at puberty[36] are almost never seen in parks. Many such girls pursue higher education (see above); but others are simply kept at home by their parents.

For girls who are subjected to suppression, violence, and attacks in the family, the park and its peer community may become the girl's main resources for support and help, and, when necessary, such a girl can quickly find from park peers somewhere to stay for some days and nights. Erupting family quarrels are a main reason girls run away from home. These are older girls who are usually well established in their "open" park peer group: their open views often give occasion for fierce debate and conflict at home.

---

36 The veiled girls are not only from very religious Muslim families: some are from liberal families, but have decided to wear the headscarf for cultural and political reasons. Some girls who have taken up the veil (occasionally against their families' wishes) have done so as a protest against US Middle Eastern policies. For many Muslims, the wish to affirm and publicly express their Muslim backgrounds was a result of the US's self-proclaimed "war against terror" following 9/11.

There is a considerable difference among the parks in the proportion of girls present. This is mostly a result of the group types meeting there, as will be shown below. And there are tendencies in the appropriation of public space, which might too readily be attributed to sex.

Girls' "Other Needs"

It is difficult to decide what the "actual" inclinations of girls and boys are, and what is formed by education and other influences. Some girls are pushed towards more sedentary lifestyles by obstructive clothing, delicate hairstyles, and long manicured nails. Further disincentives from more outgoing behavior are the repeated warnings about the numerous dangers in public, in parks, and from active play.

The other facts which keep girls from claiming space in those anyway scarce areas which are set aside for children and adolescents in cities is the rejection girls face when trying to join boys or share areas with them (see also Benard and Schlaffer 1999). Girls who use curses and stronger language, and can defend themselves (and probably are good at soccer), eventually manage better to get along with the boys in the park.

Girls – and boys as well – are exposed to dangers in public. While experimenting with their changing roles in developing from children to adults, they are likely to meet with, often considerable, difficulties. Such processes of negotiation take place, in the case of the adolescents I am concerned with here, in public space with their peers and without much guidance from parents and other adults. However, in public space they can easily escape any situation that might get out of hand.

For a girl, coming of age often means a double endangering: as adolescent, and as a woman. These dangers are projected onto her physiological structure (her female body with its "inner", hidden problematic: Helfferich 1994:45f.)[37].

Curbing girls' options for experimenting in public space are part of discriminatory and repressive child rearing practices. These include girls' (and not boys') early involvement in household tasks, restrictions on their mobility and meeting with friends, control of their physical activities (including the desire to play soccer) as well as their physical appearance (clothes), and, generally speaking, a strong emphasis on "correct behavior" regarding the family's inclinations. What is perceived as "correct" or proper behavior of course means

---

37   This implies that girls should be supported to obtain (more) knowledge about their strength, about bodily functions and practices, and about self-defence.

Cages Einsiedlerpark, "gender-sensible" design

different things in elite, (upper) middle-class, and working-class families, and varies with the family's philosophical leanings.

Many girls have internalized inculcated conservative and reactionary positions. While it is easy to blame "their families' backwardness", it is generally difficult today, with the heavily gendered marketing of life models in advertising, movies, and other mass media, to come across any alternative lifestyles for either women or men.

The debate concerning public spaces for adolescents and the obvious short-changing of girls has been aired in studies since the 1990s[38]. The park-using girls themselves often seek the support of youth workers, who have accordingly demanded space for girls, and help girls in their efforts to appropriate space. Girls' demands for more outdoor park facilities and the necessary space for activities have been supported by the Vienna municipality, and a feminist and "gender-sensitive" approach to park use has been taken up by relevant decision makers, architects, and city planners. Parks designed for girl users (geschlechtssensible Parks, Mädchenparks) have existed for more than a decade now. Planners' special emphasis is given to re-structuring the soccer cages, the most ardently defended boy-areas.

---

38   See Benard and Schlaffer (1999). See also: Förster, Gruber, Hingsamer, Mayer, Mayrhofer (2002).

d. Groups and Group Structures

„Seht ihr xy noch?" – „Naa, er ist komisch geworden!" ("You still see xy?" – "Nope, he turned strange!")

Group Formation

Some of the park groups, especially the boys', form at a very early age, often along kinship ties, by neighborhood, and according to leisure time interests, such as basketball or soccer. Children venture out to the park together, becoming established there over time. Other groups form at the adolescent stage: young people get to know each other somewhere in the city, and then meet in the park. Girls might come to their boyfriend's park, for example, as part of his group.

One group consisting of about 15 members and quite stable over the relevant decade (1997–2007) is the Seitstiegen group. We will frequently meet members of the group in the ethnography.

The Seitstiegen Group

They form a closely-knit friendship group, which can support its members in hard times, of which they all had quite a share. The group developed from a school and neighborhood peer group and comprises brothers Ja. and Mh., and Sa. and Sl., as well as Yu., Su., Ke., Il., and Sk., the sisters Sn. and Ma., then De. and occasionally Ju. – Su.'s stepsister, and two of her friends. They met in the park to play basketball, and this turned into a full-fledged friendship whose members meet regularly although many have moved away in the meantime.

A very strong factor for group formation processes is kinship. Several groups are formed around, or comprise, brothers, sisters, and/or cousins. Such relations tend to give a group a misleadingly 'ethnic' appearance: the bonding principle in such cases is family, not nationality, religion, or language.

Sometimes avoidance rules guide the relationship between brothers (the *agabey*, the older brother, must be respected by the younger, and some activities are discouraged in front of him: e.g. smoking). The ensuing rules of conduct regulate the social relations between them, and an older boy and his younger brother will be in distinct groups of age-sets. Such separate groups support each other, older brothers keeping an eye on the younger, and interfering with their conduct whenever they see fit.

Many of the groups are heterogeneous: Bosnian and Macedonian girls and boys; Turkish, Pakistani and Sri Lankan boys with Austrian girls; Roma groups from various ex-Yugoslavian countries with various religious affiliations; Iraqi, Turkish, Kurdish, and Serbian boys. There are a considerable number of seemingly ethnically uniform groups, but on closer inspection, there are many differences, depending on the categories applied. Ultimately, each group member is unique, and as such accepted in the group. And in any case, neither "ethnic" nor "religious" categories are by themselves sufficient to explain group formation, group attitudes, and group structures.

What types of groups can be met in the parks? I distinguish groups first as "tourists" and "residents" according to how they use their park. Then I distinguish the "resident" groups by whether their general attitude is "open" or "closed". I distilled my group models from long-term observations, and have found these analytic terms to be adequate[39].

Group Models

Residents and Tourists

It is necessary to distinguish between park "residents" and park "tourists". The latter are after-school recreational park users. They come in larger groups, or even alone, to the park closest to their school, during noon breaks or in the early afternoon. They play ball, or relax on benches or the lawn. They disperse after some time. The tourists cease park use with the end of their schooling, and are not this ethnography's subjects. Some of these tourists may turn into residents if they make contact with resident park groups, which might be the case if a pupil is expelled from school.

The "resident" groups are regular park users. They are there several times a week or daily and for longer times (sometimes all day). Residents almost always meet in "their" park if planning to go somewhere else as a group. They may be present at any one park for many years. Cage groups are always residents. Resident groups are in my model the park kids proper: these can be either "open" or "closed" groups.

---

39 My "open" and "closed" group models are not categories used by park groups themselves.

Open and Closed Groups

I have come to think of park groups along a continuum from "open" to "closed". These group models are fluid, and they depend on their members' attitudes, approaches, experiences, and influences, which may change quickly.

My image of groups as either open or closed is connected to their ability to move: open groups have air or space between their members. They float easily, in the parks, in the neighborhood, and through Vienna, integrating others, interacting freely, and bringing together a variety of views (boys and girls, languages, religions, nationalities, political views, economic backgrounds, sexuality). Their flexible attitude helps them to understand, to assess, and to cope with new experiences.

Closed groups' members form a rigid circle with their members predominantly interacting with each other. The group, when trying to move, meets resistance. Closed groups tend to share secrets and try to evade outside influences; some tend to sectarianism. Experiences, also of repression and violence, are dealt with within this closed system, often drawing on perceived ethnicity, nationalism, and religion. Closed groups tend to stay local, remaining in their neighborhood where they formed, often when the members were still very young. Closed groups can be either all-male or all-female[40].

Open groups tend to have a more "permeable" world-view, while the closed – "impermeable" – groups think and act along the lines of ethnic, national, and religious prejudices and self-ascriptions. Open groups welcome those who share the open view, and exclude or tend to exclude others who seem closed. Closed groups exclude, or tend to exclude, others on the basis of language, religion or gender, but are quick to accept those who share their attributes. I consider sexually mixed groups as "open" because their members accept the presence of the other sex, and interact with them.

One example of an open group is the Katzenpark group, which contains up to 20 members. One of them is Id.:

> Id. is more or less living in the park, and would constantly be there, were he not doing military service. But from there, he returns in the evening to the park almost immediately. He enjoys the large community he is living

---

40   The model of an all-male, closed group is in no way exclusive to parks, but prevails in several youth-cultural realms as well (skaters; graffiti writers; hiphoppers; break dancers; and so on). This is of course the predominant type of group in society's top layers as well.

in, with its numerous gatherings, parties, wedding receptions, and musical events. His community, Macedonian Roma from the town Pr., encompass about two thousand people in Vienna. He and his girlfriend go to the park, and to clubs and discos. He is 20 and "normal", as he says of himself. The Katzenpark group includes Ka. and his sister Sd., then Se., Er., and Ka.'s cousin Em. Loosely connected are also Bosnian girl El., Sb. – a girl with Austrian parents, and Sr., a girl from Turkish background who attends the Gymnasium (2003).

Sexually mixed groups provide the best opportunities for experience, experiment, and adventure. This does not mean that boy-girl groups are necessarily non-patriarchal: I have observed boys send their girlfriend home to change into less frivolous clothes, and brothers decide whether or not their (older) sister may come with them to the discotheque.

The parks are spatial realms where adolescents with open and closed outlooks come into intimate contact in the group members' daily interactions. Both open and closed groups know the respective others and their attitudes quite well ("wir kennen die eh'", "die sind arm", "die sind so wie wir", "ich kenne seinen Vater" – "we know them", "anyhow, they are poor", "they are like we are", "I know his father"). A basic solidarity and a feeling of social integrity and responsibility works at the park-group level.

Special Groups

Cage Groups

Cage groups – those based in a park's ball play cage – can be categorized as either open or closed. Sf.'s Weichmann Park cage group is an example of a cage group I consider "closed":

Sf. is 17, turning 18 soon, but younger looking – he is rather short, has a high-pitched voice. He spends most of his time in the park with his peers; he is crazy about soccer. Inclined to verbal abuse and physical violence, he easily loses his patience. He and his peers share a neo-national worldview. He is rarely alone, usually with his friends, the Weichmann Park cage group. Unemployed, he gets up around noon, and then meets his peers; they go to the cage to play soccer; but not always; what else do they do? Sit in the park. Sf. finds his life basically ok ("mein Leben is eh gut"). It is very hard for him to find a job. His German is not especially good, but he takes his mother to the doctor if she needs to go, and translates for her; he also picks up his little sister from kindergarten, and he loves her very much. The Weichmann Park cage is the district's best soccer cage, with a special, soft floor. The adjacent hospital and their complaints discourage playing in the evening (2005).

The fenced-in soccer cages are spaces that often serve as zones of retreat for boys and young men. They are defended against outsiders; the in-group, those in charge, those who managed to be the cage boys, see to it that nobody enters. There are certain times when the younger boy groups can play; as soon as the main group arrives, the smaller boys grant them the cage and retreat. The other park user groups, who all might have been living in the neighborhood for many years, know each other well, though are not necessarily on good terms. But if strangers arrive and want to play, someone of the cage group will usually show up and see to it that they leave again.

The groups in the cages differ in their composition. A cage in one park may have a dominant, closed cage group, but the cage in the next park probably hosts a large number of diverse groups, who all play together. Whether groups are closed or open depends on adolescents' personal attitudes and the peer group formation processes in the neighborhood.

The Seitstiegen group is a cage- and park-based open group. There is no notion of excluding the girls from the cage; the cage is fitted for playing soccer and basketball as well. However, it would be the boys who engage more often and sometimes exclusively in ball games, mainly if the girls are not there. With the girls present, they usually sit on benches together and chat.

Closed groups in soccer cages are all-male, and often uniform concerning their political world view. Two soccer teams form quickly, and the cage group organizes well around the game. Where the avoidance rules between brothers regulate such relationships, younger brothers are sometimes allowed to play with the elder adolescents. The skills of the young are commented upon, and if one of them shows a special move, it enhances his standing among his peers. Often these younger groups will be the next cage groups after their elder brothers have moved on; therefore continuity is generated, and special local histories are forged. Cage members stick together and meet in the cage even if planning to go somewhere else. Such groups, counting the younger boys as well, may average around 20 members.

Boys in the Cage

Many cage boys aspire to become professional soccer players like their role models who play in league clubs and come from the parks. Such hopes increase the importance of the soccer cage to them as they need to practice, and some do in fact start playing in a Verein (soccer club) eventually, which obliges them to lead a more regulated life and to be present at the quite demanding, and sometimes daily, training. The cages then lose importance to them as training grounds, although they still come and play with their peers. Cage group members' soccer skills can be quite remarkable, and the rough conditions improve their technique.

Within the larger group – the cage group itself – are smaller, friendship-based sub-groups. Their members spend more time together, it is a sphere of intimacy, and they share their secrets, particularly about relationships with girls, and conflicts with parents and older brothers. Boys' friendships are very strong and may form very early, sometimes at just 4 or 5 years of age; and some of these friendships are for life.

The boys in the cage groups are generally aware of their companions' life circumstances. They support each other against the "outside world" – which they encounter through such institutions as school, the police, and social welfare – and against fathers, families, and relatives who might hassle them.

Cage groups – soccer and basketball groups – can be open or closed. The following example from Flusser Park shows, how a closed group who wanted access to the soccer cage challenged resident cage groups. The subsequent violence quickly got out of hand, resulting in at least one serious injury:

> There were two groups in the Flusser Park cages: one older, all-male and open, multi-background group who played soccer, but also liked using the basketball cage right next to it; and a younger, closed group who were solely interested in soccer. Both got on well with each other: the older boys enjoyed the younger ones' respect, and also influenced them in discussions. They all were then challenged by a closed boy group of young refugees who had recently moved into the district, were in search of space to play soccer, and pursued this in a quite violent way. This led to several big fights and considerable anxiety in the two resident cage groups who were quick to ask for police support. The older, open group does not attend the cage any more – one of them got hurt badly in a confrontation, and since this group has not been a violent one, they were shocked and confused. In due course of time, however, some boys from the (former) closed refugee group occasionally came to the cage to play with the younger Flusser Park cage group. Others from the refugee group moved on as a closed group, straying further in search of new opportunities.

This example illustrates a cage as a contested space resulting from deprived groups' search for somewhere to play soccer.

For some, the cage group remains the most important social unit into the members' adult years, as this closed group from an Erdberg park:

> One all-male group, formerly park-based but now in their late twenties, still gather around one man. He is unmarried, but has his own apartment and he is economically the most successful, running several clothing production facilities and retail outlets. The others are in precarious circumstances, only temporarily employed or unemployed. They come to his home almost daily to play computer and card games, and to smoke. The host cheats at the games: the others know, but don't address this. They would not have any other place to meet – some are married, some still live with their parents, money is scarce. The group is based on dependency, and these structures have petrified over the years from the times when they started out as a closed neighborhood park and cage group.

Still from Der Freund by M. Hasaltay. Levent Sönmaz as "Osi", Sevki Arslan as Murat

Another example of adult men who still go to the park, can be seen in the short film *Der Freund* (2007), by Vienna-born artist and filmmaker Muzaffer Hasaltay. The film portrays two young men meeting at the cage in the park years after they have moved on into different lives. Their "old cage days" evoke for both the togetherness and unity formerly enjoyed. The conflict that develops between the two men, Osman ("Osi") and Murat, illustrates the consequences of violence, and how it destroys friendship[41].

There have been, over the decades in Vienna's parks and cages, closed soccer groups from a variety of backgrounds[42]. All of them share the attributes generally associated with poor urban population groups. "The cage" is a very strong identity formation site and consequently, it is very hard to "leave the cage". Members of closed cage groups are the most deprived, in terms of financial resources and access to mainstream society. They strike back against the repressions they experience by defending "their" cage against intruders: if they

---

41 The position that Bruce Lee, and martial arts in general, hold in the young men's lives is a very important feature of Hasaltay's film. See also Kato (2007).

42 At present, many closed soccer cage groups in the discussed districts are from Anatolian backgrounds.

cannot go anywhere else, then at least nobody else may enter their cage. Many cage groups share a neo-nationalist political view connected to their homeland (whatever it may be), often in reaction against the exclusion they experience. Members of closed soccer cage groups are more likely than others to react violently. The vicious circle of exclusion starts at early age and the group, often established at an early age as well, becomes ever more important as a place for support. Group-based violence seems a satisfying response to other groups, stupid teachers, prejudiced police, and racist club bouncers. Fighting, to be able to fight, to be strong, to be mean, holds some ill-defined promise. Thus essentializing and culturalizing stigmata are likely to turn into self-fulfilling prophecies through the youths' experiences of rejection, exclusion, and violence. Nevertheless, however "monolingual" such groups might seem, often boys from different backgrounds are included as well, while groups with similar backgrounds might be open and not violent at all.

A recent tendency among cage groups needs further attention:

> Cs. said that nobody went to the cage in their 3rd District Redscrew Park any more. – Where are people, the friends and peers? – In the betting café. They do not meet in the park and cage any more, nobody plays soccer now, they only bet on the games. – But, doesn't it cost a lot to be there? – No, people can hang out in there without needing to buy anything (Conversation November 2009).

Have those groups of the most deprived economic backgrounds left public space, and retreated into less accessible places, "Endstation Wettcafé"[43]? Are cages obsolete? Ulf Hannerz found in his re-visit to the Washington ghetto that the streetcorner men and their social and cultural structures, which he had so vividly described, had vanished: "The Winston Street that I had known was evidently a place in the past" (Hannerz 2004:219). Is it possible that the cage days are over?

Park Girl Groups

Apart from the girls who use parks after school or while running errands, and shift between parks, high streets, and the larger district and common urban areas, real park-based girl groups are generally still rather hard to come by; but

---

43   … as Sua Kaan's rappers Aqil and Mevlut Khan call it in their "OTK chartet" (2007).

there are some seasons when, and some parks where, park girl groups do exist. These groups are usually composed of less controlled, younger girls.

> There is a larger girl group up in the Hofpark. They're from 5 or 6 to 13, 14 years old. They spend the afternoons together in the park, in the nearby youth center, or in the park play center. Sometimes they leave the district to stray further. They live in the neighborhood, but often girls related to them come to the park from other districts to visit them. They share language and background, and some are sisters, cousins and aunts or nieces of each other. Rather evasive and secretive, they follow their own plans and ideas. They organized a quite cool winter party once: "Brooklyn im Park" in a cage, whereby they expressed their images of a "ghetto". Another time, they planned an indoor party; the flyer, kept secret from adults, showed a naked couple engaged in "petting" (2006).

This girl group is in my model a closed group because their exclusively female members share language, even family background, and outlook, and are together almost constantly. As a closed girl group they also stray further, may arrange meetings and meet people in the larger city away from neighborhood control.

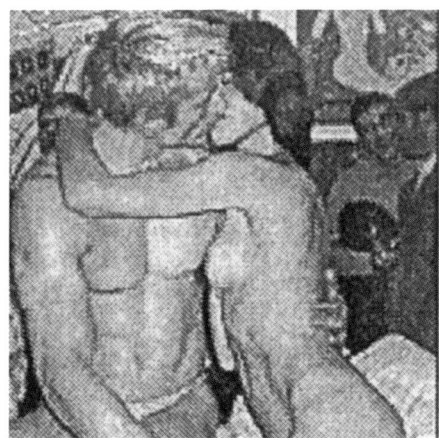

Du bist herz
Geburtsta؟
eingeladeı
Dieser Club
Jugendzeı

Party invitation

A similar park girl group existed in the Hofpark in 1999 and 2000, consisting of about ten girls between 13 and 16, sometimes including younger siblings. The group was well established and the girls were together almost constantly. Many were related to each other. As time went on, the older girls got engaged and married, and had children of their own. Two girls moved to another district. The group's park attendance gradually decreased.

Now and then, members of the girl groups come to their former park:

> I meet Mi. in the park; haven't seen her for a long time! She has three small children who now play in the cage. We talk about the old times: most of their group are mothers now. She mentions how solidarity and caring for each other had been the most important thing for all of them! The new groups now dominating the park lack this solidarity, she says. (Summer 2007).

Incipient Gangs

Incipient gangs can sometimes develop from park groups. Some of the groups take to an illegal way of life from an early age. Juvenile delinquency (violence, robbery, theft, drugs) leads some into such careers. If a group's main purpose turns into resource-acquisition, I term it an incipient gang. Incipient gangs are gangs not yet fully structured around economic goals, but headed in that direction: they are gangs in embryo ("Banden im Keim", as youth worker S. Akkilic called them), groups on their way to criminal activities but not yet beyond the stage of petty larceny – such as bicycle theft for some older guy. Though they often start as a closed group, the original bonding principle (family, neighborhood, nationality, religion, political views) gradually becomes less important, as the use of violence grows within the group. Many boys have a police record before age 14, after which they get formally busted for any offence. Assault and robbery, often committed in groups, are the most frequent crimes. Some boys can be very violent and aggressive, which sometimes results in their exclusion from their (former) peer group; but often a more violent group, or an incipient gang, will be ready to take them in.

Juvenile delinquency is not necessarily a feature of the poorest. On the contrary, a middle-class background seems to foster such tendencies:

> Again, trouble with Ys.: he stalked a girl. In the ensuing fights and chases, some of his friends show up in Flusser Park. Where did he meet them? He knows all kinds of people around town, and they are not from the district.

They are 17, but followed the girl in a car after school, showing their weapons and threatening her. One boy's father is a dentist, and he says his family is quite liberal. They are obviously up to illegal activities, and consequently avoid us from then on. Only Ys. hangs around the district's parks for a few more days, trying to find the girl, but then gets busted with a stolen moped which he tried to transport on the subway. He phones me from jail, needs help in making sense of some documents, as he is almost illiterate. However, his mother is a translator and interpreter who sometimes works for the municipality (2006).

But of course, juvenile delinquency often is a passing phase, a fact given notice in the youth law and the separate court for people below 18 years, the Jugendgerichtshof (juvenile court)[44].

Youth who start doing hard drugs, or involve themselves in other illegal activities, usually avoid contact with youth workers in the parks, or merely greet them from a distance. A few try to remain on friendly terms, but are hostile to adults' efforts at discouraging other adolescents' drug use, and this may result in a serious breakdown in the relationship between youth streetworkers and park adolescents. Eventually, contacts can be re-established by supporting and visiting the youth in jail.

Group Fission and Fusion Processes: Some Examples

Fission

In one soccer cage group Ku. began to smoke more ganja than the others, hanging out in apartments of older people who also smoked a lot. The rest of the group (one of them his brother) got worried and tried to hold him back, but he seemed to like his new life better. Slowly, he moved out of the group altogether, as they did not stop hassling him.

In another soccer cage, Ht. started questioning the nationalism and Islamism of the groups and arrived at fresh attitudes, after getting to know people with a more open view and different political approach. In many discussions with the various groups, he shaped his own attitudes more clearly.

---

44   Unfortunately, the Jugendgerichtshof is now long gone as a separate judicial institution in the 3rd District, despite strong professional and youth workers' protests against its closure. Youth trials now take place at the Landesgericht.

Eventually he moved on both spatially, as well as intellectually, away from the cage and the park.

In closed groups, fission processes are very tough. Groups are constantly engaged in discussions and debates on everyday life, football, the cage and the park, group structures, the personal conduct of members and outsiders etc., and though this might lead to a considerable amount of disagreement, the general and shared wish is to keep the group together. But if a member does leave a group, he will abandon the cage, and often the park as well.

The open Seitstiegen Park group also experienced fission processes:

The group was stable for years in their park and cage. As they grew older, they started going out together and making new friends in clubs. The Serbian brothers moved to another district, and gradually, contact with them became less frequent. New girls joined the group. The Pakistani brothers also moved away, but stayed in contact. By and by, the group left the Seitstiegen Park and cage altogether and started meeting in cafés and clubs. However, fission processes were at work all the time; people spoke critically about others due to their conduct, why he/she didn't do this or that, "he got strange", "he does not care about us any more", "she goes to different places now". The group members have moved on, finding their personal ways into society. Still, sub-groups are in closer contact, while others occasionally meet each other, and all know about their other former "parkistan" peers.

A different example from a closed Eremit Park group:

Two boys aged 15 provoked a third to snatch a woman's handbag in a busy street close to their park in the early evening. The woman, however, did not let go of her bag. All three boys came back to the park, very excited and anxious that they had been observed and followed (one wore a new white jacket). The other group members in the park did not approve of the attempted robbery at all, criticized them, and looked on mischievously. Consequently, the boys abandoned this new "career".

As mentioned before, crime is in no way an easy solution that a whole group finds to be an option for resource acquisition. Group fission and expulsion of delinquent members are frequent; and an incipient gang often forms from more ruthless ex-members of non-delinquent groups. Crime and also drugs are major reasons for fission processes. If some members of the group do not want to join, debates and discussions ensue that often end with fission of the group. Some people have to leave their groups and cages if they start to take hard drugs: they will leave the park and the district altogether and find new contacts in the drug scenes, which are open to everybody. Others return to the district and the parks in order to sell drugs to their former peers. This leads to further fusion and fission processes, depending on who becomes client and/or pusher, and who does not want to participate.

Fusion

Some fusions originate in a group's search for more, better, or different park spaces:

> A group of Serbian Roma moved from their very small park to another park. This movement was gradual, and began with a number of them playing cards on a table of the new park. This continued for the whole summer. The group was rather large and included boys and girls, smaller children and large dogs. Because they knew the people in the new park, and did not challenge the soccer cage group, things went smoothly, and everyone's acceptance gave the park a home-like feeling.

Fusion also takes place if the younger cage group, as they grow older, replaces the former group, whose members might still show up occasionally at the park:

> The older, all male, open cage group in the Flusser Park (two Kurds – one from Iraq, one from Turkey, a Shiite Iraqi boy, several Turkish boys, one Albanian from Skopje) left their cage gradually and were superseded by an all-Turkish and rather closed cage group. Members of the older group sometimes returned to play, and were always welcomed by the new, younger group.

Processes of group fusion may happen quickly, often in anticipation of a fight against intruders who challenge the park and cage groups. Sometimes fusion with older relatives occurs in "defence" against, say, groups from other districts. This may happen when a cage group or another closed group leaves their local area and goes to common urban areas, where they are bound to run into other closed groups. In the ensuing fights and quarrels, the groups find out from which park or cage their enemies originate, and go there for revenge.

Weapons might well be involved, and these fights can easily get out of hand, as happened once when a Muslim Macedonian Roma group got involved with a Turkish group from a trans-Danubian district. These came to the 5th District, and a really big fight followed, along the high street and in parks nearby, with re-runs on several Fridays and Saturdays after that. Eventually and through police and youth work interventions, the fights ceased.

A park restructuring instigated other fusion processes:

An Eremit Park soccer cage group, based on twin boys, whose soccer cage was newly designed and opened up to give weaker groups a chance to play volleyball and basketball as well, moved – after two years of considerable frustration with the new cage – to the Flusser Park, which still has its original soccer cage. They fused with the group resident in this cage, and now some boys of the combined group go to both parks and cages, others stay in the Flusser Park. But they all form a large group with a more open approach than the former groups. It is an all-male group, Anatolian with one boy from former Yugoslavia. (2000 – 2006).

These fusion processes involved groups who eventually opened up to mingle with other groups. Special fusion processes sometimes lead to the forming of larger groups of up to fifty or more adolescents.

Large Group Formation

Formation of larger groups – usually from open, sexually-mixed groups – occurs at such favorable times for fusion as spring or summer, when the weather encourages people to get together. Their gathering may then turn into movements, attracting others, meeting in or near one group's park.

The Seitstiegen group gained considerable numbers of new members as people grew up and started going out clubbing all over town, especially to clubs in the city center. New acquaintances came to visit them in their park; large groups hung out in warm summer nights until late, joking, talking, discussing, smoking pot occasionally. There were up to fifty or more adolescents – girls and boys, especially on weekends. The resulting conflicts with people from adjacent houses culminated in one 3rd floor neighbor emptying his chamber pot on the kids, who cursed back at him in rather drastic terms.

Group meetings, as this suggests, may be quite lively and loud, and do not escape the notice of neighbors. Complaints by them soon follow which are met with resistance, as adolescents do not like grown-ups to interfere with them. Such conflicts can get ugly quite fast and turn into long-term wars that include missiles, body fluids, and calls to the police. The adolescents' desire for togetherness cannot be easily fulfilled because kids are always in chronic need of money and resources. Alternative places for such meetings are hard to find for young inner city dwellers. They believe they have a right to the park and do not want to go elsewhere, but the adult neighbors cannot move out either.

A particular problem is teenage use of back streets and "Wohnstrassen" (streets with reduced traffic). Should the kids play soccer there as well, conflicts are almost programmed:

> The GaGa group in the 5th District met in such a Wohnstrasse to chat on the benches and occasionally play soccer. The adolescents, all around 16, had jobs or apprenticeships, two as cooks, one as a builder. The group attracted other young people, and they met in the evenings with their girlfriends. Their soccer play was considered a nuisance by neighbors: the ball occasionally smashed cellar windows, or was shot high in the air in what the neighbors regarded as a dangerous manner. The shouts accompanying the games were felt by the adults to disturb their peace and quiet, and watching the news on television was seemingly impossible. The conflicts between neighbors and adolescents got out of hand in the course of the spring, degenerating into threats and name-calling. Some adults even said it would be better to have car traffic again, and that the Wohnstrasse brought more troubles than the cars did. All the youth involved were working-class and had lived in the neighborhood since their early childhood; they had, just like the middle-class adult neighbors, a majority background, and both young and old all shared neo-national tendencies. – Neighborhood and block parties, suggested by youth work and organized by adolescents and adults together, defused the conflicts, at least for a limited time. (Summer 2003).

Calling Jane Jacob's neighborhood model to mind again, a good communicative base established among adults and children can be developed into positive relations, lasting also when children become adolescents, and on into adulthood. But such ideal conditions are easily imagined, and hard to establish.

Reumannplatz in the 10th District was one of the first meeting places of mainly immigration-background youth at the beginning of the 1990s, and has

been an attractive large-group gathering place for adolescents ever since. A
movement with resistance on their agenda, which included violent encounters, formed there.

The Red Brothers

The Red Brothers, who had their beginnings at Reumannplatz, were a large
group formation with a special significance. The following short history of the
Red Brothers draws upon the recollections of former adolescents and of youth
workers[45].

Parks and cages became increasingly important as meeting places to the
growing numbers of children from immigrant families who were coming of
age around the end of the 1980s. Many of these children had already started to
explore their neighborhoods in ever-widening circles; and many had formed
friendship groups. As teenagers, feeling the economic pressure of their working-class backgrounds with increasingly limited options, they responded by
meeting and hanging out together in public space and parks for games, sports,
sexual encounters, and other activities. The parks in their older, working-class,
inner city neighborhoods gave them the venue for acquiring social and other
skills (sports, culture, communication) – all important components of their
growing up.

Conflicts among park users – contested spaces in densely built-up urban
surroundings – emerged mainly around the soccer cages, but occurred also
in other areas among various user groups of diverse backgrounds. Apart from
these local processes in the parks, there was the larger urban context of the general political climate at that time: specifically, the existence of a declared rightwing, young working-class reluctant to grant positions in what they thought of
as "their" city and country. Formed as a street-based self-defence movement
against rightwing and hooligan group attacks, the first large migration-back-
ground group were the Red Brothers[46].

Ich erinnere mich, sie waren mal im Park, sie hatten rote Halstücher, oder
am Arm, und Kopftücher – und sie hatten ihre Geldbörsen mit Ketten an

---

45 I am grateful to Ercan Yalcinkaya for sharing his professional memories of "the old days".
46 On the Red Brothers and other youth groups in Vienna at that time, see the documen-
      tary film by Egon Humer, *Running Wild* (1992). Many former park kids participated,
      and today remember "the good old times". Groups in the film were the "White Lifes",
      the "Streetfighters", and many others.

"Red Brothers": Schütte-Lihotzky-Park

der Hose befestigt, Levis Hosen. Und Bomberjacken. (I remember, they came to the park once, they had red neckties, or on the sleeve, or on their heads – and their wallets were fastened to their pants with chains. Levis pants. And bomber jackets.) (Reminiscences by Ht.).

There were more than one hundred of them, and the Brothers had a general philosophy of defence against physical attacks and assaults upon them due to their often immigrant, working-class background: they saw things from a post-national perspective both regarding their own status in Vienna, because most had been born here and therefore had Austrian citizenship, and as a result of the diverse assortment of people who sided with them, which included majority Austrians, younger brothers, and a number of girls:

> Meine Schwester war bei den Red Brothers, sie war auch manchmal bewaffnet, mit Messer und so. Die jüngeren haben sich White Lifes (sic) genannt. (My sister was with the Red Brothers. She was sometimes armed, with knives and such. The younger called themselves White Lifes). (Conversation with Si. from the 15th District, 2008).

Anyway, the Red Brothers were no softies. With time on their hands, and growing strength, solidarity, and a lust for battle, the results were ever larger and uglier fights. The unrest and the violent conflicts alerted the municipality to their misguided or non-existent efforts at "integration". While "white" or non-foreign rightwing and hooligan groups had been common in Vienna, the self-empowered resistance movement of the Red Brothers and their older and younger brothers, sisters, and peers – who called themselves "White Lifes" (sic) in imitation of Los Angeles gangs and their "colors"[47] – was something new and prompted communally-funded and area-based youth streetwork[48].

Park and cage attendance increased, and parks got more recognition from the municipal authorities in the form of new equipment, more open spaces, and multiple-user designs. By 1997 the youth's park life included a large variety of groups and practices, and increasingly more people became socialized in parks. This has resulted in a large number of now adult "post-park" people who remember the old park days.

Because park groups come into existence, grow, and vanish again from public space, this is not a stable research field. My observations in this chapter were meant to establish some insight into the processes going on within and among the park groups. I have introduced some groups, and adolescents from them will be cited and described in more detail in the following parts of the ethnography.

---

47 *Colors*, a movie by Dennis Hopper (1988). Other important films for them were *Warriors, Wanderers, Boys'n'the Hood*, and *New Jack City*, as one interviewee told Egon Humer for his movie *Running Wild* (1992).

48 This was first implemented in 1992 in the 10th District (Back on Stage 10). Numerous other projects followed, resulting in the large variety of youth work now present in most Viennese districts.

e. Bodies: Some Aspects

Body Styles

There are no distinguishable park fashions or styles. Brands are known, and important to some adolescents; in general, they have a decent and cool, low-key look. Park kids rarely dress in punk, mods, rockers, or in any other "classic" youth cultural styles there might be. Soccer players are of course clad practically, sports shoes being the most important part of their clothing to them. It is not possible to identify group members by their dress (no "gang" marks): but close friends might intentionally dress similarly.

> Se. is basically content with his looks and body, „weil ich derzeit nichts mache" ("because I don't do anything at the moment" – meaning: no training or protein drinks). He wants to go to the fitness center again, to do Thai Boxing, but also to pump up his body with training and protein: „aufprotzen – es ist schöner, und den Mädels was zum anfassen bieten" ("it looks better", and he wants to offer the girls "something to grab"). „Wenn du zum Beispiel auf der Baustelle arbeitest, brauchst du kein Fitnesscenter" ("If you work at a building site, you don't need the fitness center"). He does not think he harms his body; he is not very interested in it, though: „mich interessieren Autos, das hat andere Organe, die kann man tunen" ("I'm interested in cars, they have different organs, they can be tuned"). The motor, he says, is like a heart (Interview 2005).

Solariums, fitness centers, hairdressers, barbers, clothing stores, and tattoo and piercing parlors are integral to contemporary youth consumerism – for example, to Ja. and Ke., originally from an open cage park group, as they increasingly move into urban milieus:

> "Hair is adolescents' god", colleague Hossein once said, and started his open-air park Salon Gabi, a mobile hairdresser shop where he tended to park kids' hair. One of his park customers was Ja. from the Seitstiegen Park group. Ja. looks like a male model: his eyebrows are always carefully trimmed (as he tells us of his father's); his hair is lush and long in front, and his clothes are always new and immaculately clean. He is in every respect fashion-conscious: urban hiphop, street-style, with the relevant brands, and down-dressed regarding colors and cuts.

Ke., another Seitstiegen Park group member, is obsessed with expensive haute couture, especially T-shirts and shoes. He claims to own about 30 pairs of designer brand sneakers. He is slim, and muscular from breakdancing with the Bionic B-Boys. – Each time I see him he is more tanned: his euphoria for the solarium has turned into an obsession. Upon my questions, he says, „Ja, es ist schon zuviel geworden, aber es ist so angenehm" ("Yes, it is already too much, but it is so cosy"). – My own solarium experience was on Urban Loritz Platz on a gruesomely cold and snowy Sunday. The earphones in the apparatus provided 6 different tracks of loud and fast music, while the gleaming rays pierced the body. Aha! I get the picture: it is a kind of lying-down disco. The whole ambience is adjusted to young users, among them obviously the girl working at the counter (2006, 2009).

These consumption places include fitness centers and sports clubs, which are mainly in the common urban areas: one must leave the neighborhood to get to them, and access is costly and good conduct required. These places, part of the adult world of consumption, become important for some adolescents when about 15 or 16 years old, and increasingly so as they grow older and have some money. The relevant body styles and practices are an integral part of the consumer-based lifestyle sported in common urban areas and has, for park kids, become an expression of belonging to the larger urban youth scenes and crowds who share the opinion that attitude, not ethnicity are the relevant factors for being cool.

It must have been around 2006 when I first noticed that break-dance was less interesting to the B-Boys; Su. increasingly often carried a sports bag with him, and mentioned going regularly to a fitness center on Mariahilfer Strasse.

New experiences in such places can be termed consumption-oriented initiations, including body-related experiences, symbolized in styles and in attitude. Boys from poorer cage groups do not have enough money to share these looks, and for closed groups mainly interested in soccer, style is not very important anyway. And it is hard for them to conform to the urban crowds in clubs, malls, and shopping areas. But as soon as they wish to take part in urban pastimes like clubbing, they find that both their modes of dress as well as their closed attitudes are unwelcome in clubs and discos.

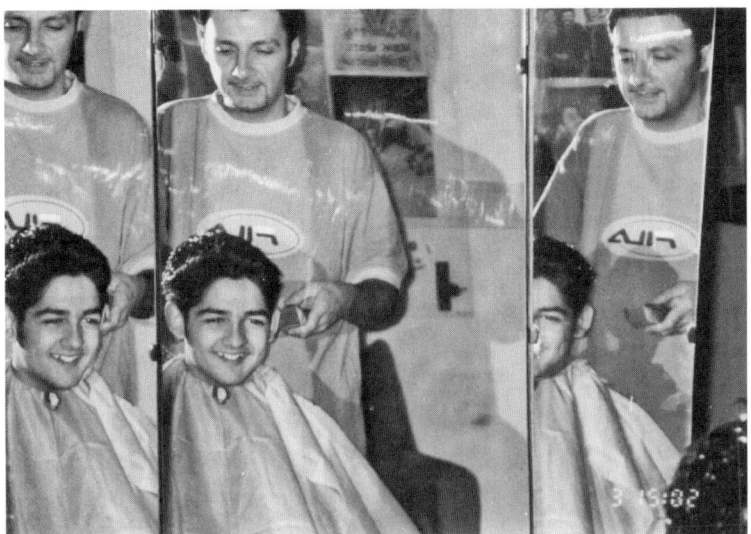

Salon Gabi: Hossein and Novica

One Erdberg cage group in the mid-1990s chose, for their clubbing evenings, satin clothes and narrow pants, with silken shirts. This style – taken
from TV mafia series – was not well received by club bouncers, especially
since the boys dressed this way tended to show up in groups, and reacted violently to any critique.

But park groups not only pick up on television styles; *vice versa*, urban street
styles often become fashionable in mainstream couture and the fashion world.
Park youth thus both copy and set trends. Open groups tend to be much more
fashion- and style-conscious than closed groups, and they decidedly wish to
differentiate themselves from racists, uncool people, and brutes.

Helena Wulff stated, "Most of the girls' consumption was directly connected to their *bodies*, and they cultivated their own esthetic of ethnic equality
through their youth styles" (Wulff 1995:72f., italics in original). This is especially the case for older Viennese adolescents who have more resources and
mobility, and spend more time in the common urban areas among larger urban crowds and scenes. They participate in the urban consumption patterns
with their choice of messages, as certain brands, styles, and symbols signify the
rejection of neo-national and anti-immigration positions. Such signs change

quickly, and many are appropriated by others who like them, and therefore change their significance and message.

As to self-confidence regarding their looks, the adolescents expressed no great desire for change in physical appearance – at least in 2005 when I interviewed them. The respondents were self-confident in, and content with, their looks – some boys wanted to become more muscular, and the girl wanted to lose weight. It seems that being part of a peer group – as all park kids are – certainly helps their self-view. One declared religious adolescent, Sf., was sure that he was "meant to be like I am", and there was no need to change that. Ae. said, "was wär ich dann, so ein Typ der sich selbst erschaffen hat" ("What would I be, a guy who created himself?"), something which he rejected to be.

This seems to be changing rapidly. Recently, cosmetic surgery is becoming more popular with park youth:

> Cs. said that one young man from a park group in the 3rd District is rumoured to have invested his gambling winnings in cosmetic nose surgery. According to his friends, „Die Nase war vorher absolut in Ordnung. Seither haben wir ihn nicht mehr gesehen." ("The nose was absolutely ok before. We haven't seen him since.") (November 2009).

Further research on adolescents' body concepts and images is necessary, but it is obvious that the heavy mass marketing of cosmetic surgery has brought such options to young people's notice. While usually lacking the money, even a park boy can come across the necessary sum by a lucky game.

> Another recent development is the increasing interest that older adolescents and young men have in bodybuilding. They speak of protein shakes, "testo" shots, the specific training of muscle groups, and are obsessed with their "lat" (latissimus), sixpack, and legs (according to Cs., 2011).

And there are hints that girls are especially victimized by mediated body images: during youth work-initiated girls' picnics in parks, where food and nutrition could be discussed, it appeared that some girls were embarrassed to eat in front of others. Some were afraid of eating too much, and tried to eat as small portions as possible. Several girls said that their boyfriends wanted them to be slim, and scolded them if they ate at all. The girls also seemed to be uninformed about healthy foods, and how to prepare them.

Food

> Sa. from Seitstiegen Park often goes out to eat, but „zu Hause kocht Mama"
> ("at home, Mama does the cooking"). He can cook himself (eggs, spaghetti,
> Griessnockerlsuppe), „es ist aber Frauenarbeit" ("but it is women's work"). –
> Weichmann Park Sf.'s mother does the cooking at home, and Sf. himself can
> cook as well: *melemen*, potatoes, other simple things. But he often eats "draus-
> sen" (outside): kebab, pizza. – Ke. is a fan of military food, „das beste Essen
> von ganz Österreich" ("Austria's best food"), and he thinks regular eating is
> very good, very healthy. He would like to gain a bit of weight. – Ae. always
> goes out to eat after getting up late. He eats fast food, including traditional
> Viennese fast food. He tries to avoid his mother at home, if possible (2005).

Everybody from the parks eats fast food, and many not just occasionally but
on a daily basis: hamburgers, pizza, schnitzel, and kebab. Even when food is
available at home but cannot be easily warmed up or is not to their liking, they
go out for fast food. Adolescent boys bring their own take-away food home
late at night to eat in front of the TV. Or they fry up some eggs in the kitchen
after coming home from work or the park. Breakfast is often eaten very late,
sometimes after noon, when the youngsters get up after everybody else has left.

Family meals were not mentioned at all during the nine interviews in 2005.
The de-structuring of daily life due to unemployment or erratic working hours,
as well as the dissolution of working-class families' joint activities, have led to
a "self-service food culture" in the homes where every family member consults
the fridge after coming home.

> De., aged 17, a female member of the Seitstiegen Park group, does shopping
> and cooking if her mother and younger brothers are on holidays. She quite
> enjoys it; but she also cooks for the family often anyway (Interview 2005).

> Su. lives in a students' home where he shares his room with another boy,
> who works as a cook. Su. says that they often cook together, and like it a lot.
> He learned it from his father, but also has some experience from his own
> work in the gastronomy and in the catering business (2005).

De. and Su. are exceptions among park adolescents, who largely feed on fast
food available on the streets near the park neighborhoods. They are both older,
and picked up cooking (and shopping) from their father or mother. All the
others are increasingly dependent on fast food or their parent's cooking and

shopping. Medical doctor B. Schindlauer remarks, "Ein immer grösser wer-
dendes Angebot an Fast Food Möglichkeiten und ein unausgewogenes Koch-
verhalten zu Hause drängt die Jugendlichen immer mehr in eine ungesunde
Ernährung" ("The increasing fast food options on offer, and poorly-balanced
cooking at home, pushes the adolescents more and more towards an unhealthy
diet", Schindlauer 2008:59).

As I have no control group data (of non-park-based adolescents), I cannot say whether or not park-group adolescents do have an especially unhealthy
lifestyle. However, B. Schindlauer sees the park youth's nutritional habits – together with their smoking and increasingly sedentary leisure time activities –
as definite health risk factors (Schindlauer 2008:64).

Health

> Sa.: „Ich lebe eh gesund, mit Ecstasy und Kokain, haha, ein Scherz". ("I'm liv-
> ing healthy anyway, with Ecstasy and cocaine, haha, a joke.") (Interview 2005.)

Health issues are not very high on the park youths' agenda of knowledge and interest. Younger park kids' health behavior was researched by B. Schindlauer (2008).
He describes their practices to be problematic due to various reasons. As for older
adolescents (from 17 to 20 years), my observation is that they increasingly feel bad
because of job stress on one hand or unemployment stress on the other.

Park adolescents' health is largely determined – apart from their own health
behavior – by the urban surroundings they dwell in. Headaches, stomach troubles, and general bad health are largely caused by unhealthy surroundings both
in the park and in their homes. Risk behavior in sports on dangerous grounds,
accidents, neglected colds, unhealthy diet, smoking at a very young age, and
more add to the physical stresses inherent in the urban surroundings.

The youths' knowledge about the human body is varied, but usually quite
limited, for example centered on muscle groups and how to train them. There
are not many obese kids in the park – they all move about quite a lot, especially
the soccer- or basketball-playing youths – but if they outgrow park life and turn
to a more sedentary leisure lifestyle (with increasing time in front of computers, TV screens and play stations, as well as in cars and betting cafés), their
health will probably deteriorate, and their information about healthy foods
and diets is scarce. This is confirmed by Schindlauer's data.

The urban park adolescents have not much information on the countryside
around Vienna – apart from several majority kids who have grandparents in
rural areas – and know not much about recreation through hiking, climbing,

Fast Food Place, Währing

skiing, and so on. They lack knowledge about plants and animals – the natural surroundings – and often cannot even identify the types of trees, shrubs, and flowers in the parks.

> Going to the countryside with park groups to a basic wooden hut in alpine Styria always was great fun. Making a fire and roasting sausages and potatoes was very much enjoyed. However, the black nights usually frightened the kids – even, or especially, the "bad boys" from an incipient gang. They also were totally ignorant about how to find one's way in the woods. Collecting mushrooms and berries was new to them, as was firing the stove in the hut's kitchen.

Sports other than soccer, basketball, and occasionally breakdancing or park acrobatics are rarely among the park kids' pastimes. Su. plays cricket with his Sri Lankan friends. Some older boys and young adults are interested in the martial arts and in boxing and kick-boxing, and attend the numerous training parlors.

But I found that the park kids' access to health services (doctors and hospitals) is good, and that they are aware of and acquainted with the city's health-care services. They know the large hospitals and their emergency wards; and all interviewed adolescents had a family doctor they said they'd turn to in case of illness.

Love and Sexuality

"I am solo, with many girlfriends" says Sa., 17, who is soft-spoken and friendly, and most of the time in a good mood. He always had had girlfriends, even
when he was very young. He says to wake up in the morning, and the girl is
not there, makes him feel lonely. However, once he has enough, he is very
quick to end the relationship (2005).

Some kids can trust their parents, and are allowed to bring girlfriends or boyfriends home for the afternoons, or are allowed to sleep over. The kids will of
course also take advantage of any absences of their parents and other family
members to have girl- or boyfriends at home. Park-based mixed groups promote sexual interactions between group members, and relevant experiences
are embedded in the group and talked over with the peers.

Ke. and his girlfriend Mt. often hang out in his room at his parent's place;
he says that her father is not entirely enthusiastic about him because he sees
him as a Turk, and that they therefore avoid her parents' home. Both are in
the Seitstiegen Park group, and interested in music, especially hiphop and
urban R'n'B, and go out to clubs with their peers, her elder sister Sn. among
them (Interview 2005).

Open park youth groups who live an urban style not centered around "ethnicity"
but based on shared values and interests, may face difficulties with their parents
who are doubtful about their children's open views and their relationships.
Ra. was a basketball player in Flusser Park, and went to the park with his
peers and sometimes with his sisters and younger brother, and his father came
with them occasionally. They are from middle-class Karachi family backgrounds. Ra., however, was not a long-time regular in the park, and later merely
came to the open-air hiphop parties until he travelled to Pakistan, the US, and
Germany. His experience with love was painful:

Ra. was recently left by his Vienna-based German girlfriend; her feelings
were not as strong as his. Also, her parents did not accept him because he is
a Muslim, „die kennen so was nicht", "they don't know anything like that".
Anyway, his parents were not sure either, hesitant … but his mother had
sewn Pakistani clothes for her. His sad experience has acutely influenced his
opinions of – as he sees them now – 'mixed' relationships. He says, "Love-
sickness is a European problem … Pakistan, Saudi Arabia are different. The

girls are brought up differently, family-oriented." He says that he loves independent women, but shares the Pakistani mentality. „Spasskultur nervt,
Heirat ist nicht nur Liebe, wenn die Liebe nachlässt, kommen die Kompro-
misse. Ehrlich, nach meinen Erfahrungen möchte ich zurück nach Karachi und dort heiraten." ("Fun culture is a nuisance: marriage isn't just love.
When love fades, then compromising starts. Honestly, after my experiences I want to go back to Karachi and get married there.") (Interview 2003).

Ra.'s feelings were badly hurt, which pushed him towards what he perceived as
'his own culture' and its, as he felt, honesty and mutual compromising in relationships. He had experienced these attitudes in his open-minded family, who
have lived in Vienna for a number of years. He now associates these values with
the broader culture of Sunni marital practices, which he sees as supporting and
emotionally mature.

In some open groups that are sexually mixed but guided by ideas of male
dominance, the girls are restricted and controlled by either brothers or boyfriends. Boys order girls to stay at home while they go out with their friends,
decide when they can join them in an evening out, and what they should wear.
In the park, the boys protect their sisters and girlfriends, which is the condition
under which they are permitted to be in the park. Their relationships are likely
to be restricted to the group, which is based on family ties, and the boyfriend
has to be approved of by the girl's brother.

> Bu., a 14-year old girl who was rather rude in her language and more than
> able to defend herself against any encroachments, told me that she had met
> a boy at the swimming pool in Simmering. She had given her mobile phone
> to him so that he could screen her calls to prove that she has no other boy-
> friend. She says that she likes him to be jealous like that (2006).

Bu. is a very independent girl who, together with her (girl)friends, widely
roams the city. Her mobility enabled her to meet her new friend, who was at
the swimming pool with his group. Bu. and other girls share the reactionary
and patriarchal view of the boys, and even seem to be proud of their boyfriends' possessive attitude.

Some girls go along with these attitudes, especially if these are consistent
with their upbringing, in which they might be accustomed to a brother's well-
meant and kind control. Such girls' expectations of a boyfriend are that he, like
a brother, should take responsibility for her. A clash of attitudes sometimes

occurs if an open-minded girl encounters a boy from a closed group. If experiencing the restrictions on her personal freedom and mobility in such relationships, she will end it and thereafter avoid the boy and his group if she can. This may lead to considerable stress, conflicts, and even stalking and violence, and many girls are wary of meeting such a boy – one reason why girls are underrepresented in parks where closed group boys dominate the scene. Certain parks, cages, and boy groups have bad reputations with the girls.

Cage boys from closed groups who begin to get interested in girls must leave their cage to meet any: they go to the local youth centers, or frequent malls. Cage boys often lack the money, appearance, and behavior necessary for going to the "better" places. And they might be banned from the youth center or the mall because of fighting, rowdyism, or other forms of misconduct. So when a boy sees a girl he fancies, or a girl is interested in him, he will try to approach her without his peers present, perhaps on the street.

The growing into gender roles during adolescence involves the testing of certain models of relationships. A park boy who does succeed in getting to know a girl does not want to bring her to the park, but prefers to take her somewhere else. It is not common among "closed" cage boys to bring a girlfriend to the park. They do not consider the parks, or their peers, as suitable for a girl:

> Ht. went home from the park. On the street he saw, at some distance, an older park boy with a girl and greeted him with a jovial nod. The other boy did not react. Next day, in the park, that guy tried to hit him! He was furious at Ht.: "Never do this again, greet me with respect, you idiot! That was my fiancée!!" The girl had just arrived from Anatolia (1995).

If a family wishes to find a suitable spouse for their son, they might try back in their home village or town (see also Mayer 1994). Such relationships may be quite important to both partners and lead to marriage. This marks the end of the park boy's adolescence and his status among the friends is different. He will still meet his park peers, but not many will bring the spouse[49].

---

49 This parallels Hannerz's and Liebow's findings from the 1960s ghetto streetcorner society: it does not influence a man's social behavior whether he is single, married, or has a girlfriend. Similar information comes from W.F. Whyte in his *Street Corner Society*: "Furthermore, it is easy to overlook the distinction between married and single men. ... married or single, the corner boy can be found on his corner almost every night of the week" (1943:255).

A particular reason some boys have for tolerating girls in the park is sex. The girls involved are not the boys' girlfriends, but other girls, sometimes older, interested in sexual activities. Park and cage boys who cannot meet "nice" girls need to stray further, to such uncontrolled areas as the Prater. It is the tougher girls whom they will meet there, sexually experienced and used to handling situations with boys.

Sexual activities take place in parks and interstitial spaces. Both boys and girls are keen on these experiences and experiments; but the power relations in sexual park activities are often in favor of the males. This can involve misuse, exploitation, verbal abuse, and sometimes rape. Forms of exploitation include taking pornographic pictures of the girl and circulating or selling them. Usually groups are involved in these sexual activities, at least from the boys' side; the girls are often in pairs.

But there is a certain amount of imaginative embellishment to the stories and rumours as well. Boys and girls want to explore sexuality, and long for these experiences. A public neighborhood park is not necessarily the worst place for experimenting: it is well-known territory, and the adolescents usually know each other. Rumours, horror stories from their friends and other girls and boys, and warnings from parents might backfire and push girls (and boys) into sexual encounters in remote, anonymous places which might ultimately prove more dangerous: private cars and apartments, clubs, and far-away parks without people nearby.

Sex is also a way some boys and girls make money. Working at nightclubs as a waiter or waitress, being a good dancer and offered a promotion to go-go dancing (sometimes in golden cages), and other 'options' in nightclubs and entertainment places make the transition to prostitution smooth and easy for adolescents with an interest in dancing, the desire for sexual experiences, and the need to earn money. There is a vast field for research here; but this study is one of park youth, and only brief notice can be given to their extended activities.

Drugs

Tobacco

8 of 9 interviewed adolescents between 17 and 20 smoke daily, regularly. Only one of them wants to quit. The boy who does not smoke at all plays soccer in a club (Interviews 2005).

Most adolescents in parks smoke cigarettes, some having started even before they were 10 years old. B. Schindlauer interviewed 12 adolescents in Margareten's parks in 2006, and found that "10 of the 12 adolescents smoke. Only two girls … don't, all of the boys smoke. They started smoking between 10 and 13 years of age and have smoked increasingly more since then. … 10 to 30 cigarettes a day" (Schindlauer 2008:42, translated by DM).

Tobacco and alcohol are the dominant legal drugs in Austria. However, the use of alcohol is much more varied in the parks than the ubiquitous abuse of cigarettes.

Alcohol

Se. (18) smokes up to one pack a day, and rarely drinks more than one beer; at parties mostly soft drinks and Tequila. „Nicht mit jedem kann man trinken, die machen Blödsinn. Aber ich kenne die Leute, ich passe mich an." ("You can't drink with everybody, they do stupid things. But I know people, I adjust to them") (Interview 2005).

There are surely bad experiences behind Se.'s remarks (his own stupid things, maybe). But park kids are critical towards the alcohol-drinking mainstream society around them. Se. and others of the park youths are of various Muslim backgrounds, but we cannot simply assume that neither they nor their families drink[50], while some non-Muslim majority youths also regard alcohol as despicable. Influential hiphop crews, for example, completely abstained from tobacco, alcohol, and other drugs[51]. The techno movement refrained from alcohol: they took Ecstasy instead. Some marijuana smokers look down on alcohol drinkers.

---

50 Of course there are diverse alcohol cultures in the immigrants' countries: national, subcultural, and working-class practices.

51 E.g. the Zulus from Vienna's Grossfeldsiedlung, a trans-Danubian housing project, who are oriented toward Afrika Bambaata's 1970s and 1980s groups in the Bronx. On Bambaata and the Zulu Nation, see David Toop (1994, especially pp. 86ff.).

It is necessary to observe the alcohol use among park youths. Schindlauer found that "especially boys are very reserved in their use of alcohol; but for girls too, it is not particularly popular" (2008:42, transl. by DM); and also my experiences with, and observations of, the park groups indicate that alcohol is not an important drug to them, with some temporary and/or individual exceptions.

> Some say they used to drink a lot but now not any more, not like they used to, and arrived at a moderate use which is strictly social, ranging from "sometimes a small beer", to "one or two beers when going out". One says that he does not drink at all due to religious reasons, while one says his weekend pastime is *Saufen*: heavy drinking (Interviews with nine adolescents, summer 2005).

There are other experiences, of course:

> A fairly unusual incidence involved a girls' group (13 years old) who smuggled lots of so-called Alkopops on an excursion into the country, where they got drunk quite quickly and suffered fits of violence and self-destruction, including suicidal passion. They were all Austrian majority girls, loosely affiliated with the Seitstiegen Park group, but not necessarily regulars at the park. They used to go to the *Nachtschicht*, a huge trans-Danubian majority youth discotheque[52]. Koma-Saufen (binge drinking) is program there, and alcohol is at times ("happy hour") ridiculously cheap (Summer 2001).

Coma (binge) drinking is clearly part of some groups' coming of age in Vienna's majority working-class culture. It also seems to be a major leisure time activity in Austria's small towns and countryside. But it is not mentioned by, nor observed very often in the park groups. Although many start going out to clubs when only 10 or 11 years old, drinking is not their main interest. Some have experiences with the alcoholism of fathers or mothers, which might cause them to drink themselves, or else turns them off completely from alcohol – difficult to say which response prevails.

> Sf.: "Alcohol? Never. It is forbidden!" (Interview 2005). – Yu. from the Seitstiegen group even refrains from using hair gel containing alcohol.

---

52 *Nachtschicht* (night shift) recently changed its working-class name to the trendier *Club Couture*.

Declared Muslim adolescents for whom religion has taken on a strong importance and meaning (neo-Muslim religiosity) strictly adhere to the prohibition against alcohol. Others who have not taken to fundamentalist Islam but who would in any case defend their Muslim beliefs, experiment with this mainstream drug occasionally:

> On one cold evening in November 2005 a reporter from television was scheduled to come with a camera team to interview some park boys; production of the news report was in context with the riots in Parisian *banlieus*. My colleague Gina and I had telephoned the Flusser Park cage boys and asked them to come to the office to be interviewed and filmed. They appeared, from the park, euphoric and drunk! They said that it simply was the day to get drunk. We go to the Seitstiegen Park for the shooting. Ys. appears, not drunk, but crazy as always – they all scream into the camera: „Wir wollen Waffen und Weiber!" ("We want weapons and women!")[53].

Some adolescents get drunk in the park once or twice, like the Muslim boys (between ages 14 and 17) in the incident described above. Some park youths try drinking for some time; and many of the older youths said that they drank in earlier times:

> Ht. says that he and his cage group – park kids in Erdberg in the 1990s – tried out alcohol when they were 15, 16 years of age. They saw other people drinking and decided to try it as well. They took to "stuff we knew from TV – whisky, vodka, rum". They drank in the park or in apartments of friends whose parents were away. They would get sick, vomit, came home drunk. When older, they had cars to go to the large discotheques on Vienna's outskirts. One of them always stayed sober to drive. – Car owners were wary of the police, and feared for their driving licence and their cars, especially as they often planned to go to Turkey by car in summer.

---

53 To appear in the media is to disappear in the media: "one cannot appear in 'the media' in one's true subjectivity", as Peter Lamborn Wilson aka Hakim Bey stated (Media Creed for the Fin de Siecle, www.hermetic.com/bey/pw-creed.html). Stuart Hall also comes to mind, with his media critique that, if working-class people appear in the mass media, it is only related to "problems", but never from their point of view of the story (The Chronicle, archive 01-08.101. See also "Black Men, White Media", 1974).

For them, cars, clubs, and girls were more important than getting drunk. Mobility enabled them to frequent large discotheques, further away; but conspicuous consumption back home – showing off the new car in Turkey – was the dominant desire. And owning a car is surely many park boys' dearest wish.

Most park adolescents have experiences with the bums, drunkards, and homeless who also hang out in the parks. The kids sometimes criticize them and get into arguments with them when they are drunk and aggressive, especially if they scare children. But the park kids also interact with them on friendly terms.

> Cs. tells about the homeless and bums in his park. "There used to be Franz, Frankie and Anton, we knew them, and talked occasionally. They drank wine from these cheap packs already in the morning. They are all gone; the guys that come now don't speak German, they're Polish, I think" – but they still interact with them, sometimes share cigarettes on park benches (Conversation November 2009).

Initiation into a society's dominant drug(s) is surely one of the developmental tasks of adolescence. Many majority kids try to come to terms with alcohol, often by binge drinking. Park youths find modest recreational use generally ok, but as Se. says: "You cannot drink with everybody".

To go into this a bit deeper, it is helpful to draw on sociologists Eisenbach-Stangl, Bernardis, Fellöcker, Haberhauer-Stidl and Schmied (2008) and their analysis of alcohol in Austrian traditional culture, and the initiation into its use in highly visible juvenile alcohol scenes. The groups of marginalised and conspicuously drinking youths and youth groups are mostly boys of non-migrant background (2008:15). The authors maintain that the male character of immodest alcohol use is both internationalized (at least in industrialized countries), and anchored in Austrian festival tradition. Drinking as an indication of adulthood is also part of the legal system as "Trinkmündigkeit" (being of age to drink), and therefore connected to other realms of adulthood, such as political representation, legal responsibility, and driving. The authors argue that such alcohol scenes are the most important, probably even the only, public initiations into gender roles: young men show strength through heavy drinking, in the drinking games, through buying rounds, by outbursts of violence, and also by ruthlessly approaching girls. Intensive alcohol consumption is not part of the young women's gender role, but nevertheless drinking does have its place in their repertoire, attracting and meeting men (Eisenbach-Stangl et al. 2008:177f.).

Alcohol use is doing gender, but also doing social, because community and sociability is forged, and in the included rituals, these scenes compete publicly; the common social situation of the group members is expressed. But juvenile alcohol uses are also variations of the new leisure-scenes of post-traditional societies, and the authors find that the contemporary juvenile alcohol scenes are new in one respect: they have been penetrated by commercialized leisure enterprises which increasingly shape and even dominate the public tastes and desires (Eisenbach-Stangl et al. 2008:179).

From my observations and park youths' statements, their occasional alcohol consummation fits into this new, commercialized use of alcohol transported by media and movies. The traditional Austrian festival culture does not attract youths of immigrant background – but commercials do. However, I cannot say here if, or in what ways, park youth identify with traditional alcohol cultures of their former homelands, such as Turkish and Anatolian, Roma, and 'Balkan' festival cultures, or working-class drinking habits.

Generally, as Eisenbach-Stangl and her co-authors maintain (2008:38f.), drug consumption practices are relevant forms of social representation and of presenting subjectivity through symbolic dimensions of consuming drugs. So while alcohol as such is not important (presently) for park-based crowds, the preference for other drugs and their respective symbolic connotations are interesting.

Cannabis

At the beginning of the new millennium, there was a time when the Vienna Green Party advocated the legalization of cannabis. This was a period when park kids showed a lively interest in this party. The topic came up with our *Park Wahlen Projekt* and the adolescents' *Parklament*, which were complements to school and pupils' parliaments[54]. Other indications of adolescents' interest surfaced in self-organized youth group discussions for Park TV, in which drugs were the predominant issue.

---

54 *Park Wahlen, Parklament,* and Park TV were projects initiated by and realised with park kids by mobile youth work.

Presently, the most interesting substance for park groups is cannabis[55]. Many older park groups, who tend to use it on into their adult years, smoke "weed" and hashish, though use is curbed by lack of money. Smoking is also, due to being illegal, seldom admitted openly (see also Schindlauer 2008).

> In summer of 2007, the younger Eremit Park boy group's interests circled mainly around cookie recipes and how to bake them, which they eagerly tried to memorize – an interest quite far off their tracks, if not for the hashish-enhanced dough.

In his chapter "Cannabis as a Cultural Style", ethno-botanist Terence McKenna (1999:154ff.) maintains that cannabinoids place "a person in intuitive contact with less goal-oriented and less competitive behavior patterns", and thus could be seen as a substance furthering group feelings of solidarity. Other effects are increased fantasies, utopian visions, hilarity, and mellowness. Music and visual impressions are perceived more intensely.

> We started smoking weed in the park; then we went to where it could be bought. Such small cafés changed very often, opened up and closed down again. We liked the atmosphere in these places, there was a mixture of people, and they were less aggressive, not like in the drinking parlors. It was a laid-back mood, and we also enjoyed the music there, we stopped listening to mainstream techno, started to become interested in other stuff, like British trip-hop … and somehow smoking seemed connected to black people, who we felt close to, and to a vague image of 'ghetto'. (Memories from the mid-1990s).

Apart from the connotation with black culture and images of a ghetto[56], some park groups also put cannabis into context with an imagined "Orient": Sufis traditionally use the drug, and the kids are aware of the fact that the homelands and major producing areas of cannabis are (or were) India, Afghanistan, and Muslim countries around the Mediterranean.

---

55 Chicago sociologist Howard Becker has provided us with the in-depth study *Outsiders* (1963), where he discusses use of cannabis, and describes and analyses the initiations involved in "becoming a marihuana user".

56 These vague images of "ghetto" are shared by many park youths; see also Rakic (2010) on the term's connotations for Viennese rappers.

Heroin

The misuse of heroin had great importance in the parks towards the end of the 1990s, with occasional later flare-ups.

> Xx., 17, a former soccer player with the junior set of a renowned club, encountered hard times with hard drugs. Becoming a pusher to finance his habit, he soon got into trouble everywhere, and terrorized his mother for money. He frequented the parks less often, but kept drug-dealing contacts with some youth of the district.

People who start using hard drugs usually leave the parks and their group to move into the larger urban drug scenes. These scenes "have room for everyone", as drug streetworkers say. In the scene, the supply of drugs is organised, and all social, emotional, and economic ties are structured through and around the drugs and their equally addictive substitutes.

Further discussion on the use of heroin exceeds the scope of this study, as presently users do not make up significant numbers in Viennese park groups (apart from adult users who occasionally go to the public park toilets). Cocaine, not a major issue in the parks because it is too expensive for the park kids' small purses, is occasionally mentioned in conversations, particularly because of its glamorous appearance in movies and on television.

Music as Experience

Musical experience is a human universal, and music and dancing are intimately connected with youth experiences. While music – melody and rhythm – influences the emotions directly, lyrics are poetry, opening new conceptual and imaginative worlds. Music synthesizes the affective and emotional with the intellectual, expressing them in physical sensation, and often in song and dance. Music, and especially its performance, involves the whole person: feeling and knowing, experiencing and reflecting are linked.

Teenagers began to be target groups for music marketing in the USA in the 1950s, when the "baby boomers" were coming of age and had some money on their hands (Szatmary 1991). Developing one's own approach to music, discovering new styles, becoming interested in new musical forms is surely one feature of growing up today. Adolescents in the present-day global consumer society find increasingly many musical styles and interpretations that are accessible via the worldwide net.

Kids' Showcase at "The Beach" 2001

Park youth are no exception regarding their interest in music, and music holds promise for a future career for them, as many of the musical stars – singers, rappers – are from working-class and also a ghetto background. Such hopes appear more real than the hazy universes of the labor market.

Opportunities to sing and play are enthusiastically seized by the park kids[57]. They perform anywhere they can, no matter how small or large the audience: rap and beatboxing battles, singing solo or with a group, karaoke, bands, folklore dances.

Sd. is a regular at Katzenpark. She is Ka.'s elder sister, and they spend much time together. Their family belongs to the Macedonian Roma community, and their park has been a main meeting point for the generations, who an-

---

57 I have organized, and participated in organizing, several show programs at large park festivals where park kids performed on stage. At the *10 Years Back on Stage* Show Case on Reumannplatz (2002), the following acts appeared: Die Kleinen Talente; The Three Angels; Blood In – Blood Out; Makedonia; Harman; Jelena and the B-Girls; No Pain and Fresh B.; Dirty Drunkyn Brothaz; Karakan; B Boys Soul Style; B Boyz Crew; The Devils.

nually celebrate the Parkfest, organized by the park groups themselves, at which Sd. acts as a host and master of ceremony, announcing the musicians and introducing people to each other. Music groups play live, and there is ample room for musical happenings as young singers and rappers appear on stage. It is also a veritable neighborhood party with young and old dancing the *kolo*, a traditional circle-dance; and recurring guests are the bellydancers from an adjacent dance studio class.

Musical Styles

Globally Mixed

Ra. listens to hiphop and also Bhangra, mixed with hiphop beats. The parties he likes are at the Volksgarten Pavillon and the P1 in Vienna's First District. These parties are frequented by a mixture of people – "white women in Saris, Indian girls wearing trousers", as he relates. He also went to such parties in the USA during his one-year stay with relatives (Interview 2003).

Many kids listen to the globally distributed Anglo-American black music like hiphop, modern R'n'B and soul. First-class hiphop DJ sets have been played in parks[58], for example by "Demon Flowers" Werner Geier, grand doyen of Vienna hiphop who prematurely died in 2007; and also by internationally well-known and famous DJ DSL, long-standing radio MC Sugar B., DJ Hossein "Mastercash", and by hiphopper Zuzee (from the major label act Waxolutionists)[59].

DJ Mastercash, well acquainted with park life, has brought modern R'n'B and park youth together at the Volksgarten Club, a fancy inner city location with a longstanding tradition. Mastercash's parties and clubbings – *SmoothTalkin'* every Friday from the mid-90s on, *Juicy* on Saturdays – formed an all-Viennese youth scene, comprising mainly older teenagers from varied and often immigration backgrounds, from Vienna's international elite schools and from the parks. The easy, cool, luxurious and cosmopolitan atmosphere was enabled also by a very strict door policy that segregated "good" and "bad" kids, "in" or "out". It was not easy to pass the gates, and once inside, eventual troublemakers were evicted consistently and without mercy.

---

58 Organised by Christoph Möderndorfer for *Back on Stage* mobile youth work, especially from 1996 to 2001.
59 On reception of hiphop in Vienna see Gächter (2000).

"Demon Flowers" Werner Geier and Urbs, Check den Park 1997

DJ Zuzee

Young park people who attended the Volksgarten clubbings certainly belonged to open groups, and their general social background was more middle-class, their families liberal and open-minded as well, with a life in a relatively sound economic situation. Some knowledge of English enabled them to understand the modern R'n'B lyrics; some group members had been to the US, visiting relatives, and had either worked, or attended high school there.

Depending on their language background, young park people listen to Turkish pop and arabesk, Yugoslavian "Jugo" and "turbo" pop, and Bhangra and Bollywood film music. Ke.'s and Yu.'s musical tastes are good examples of an open park group's preferences in 2003:

> Ke. from the Seitstiegen group speaks Turkish with his parents, and German with his younger sister. He has a Viennese girlfriend. His music: hip-hop, but he is not interested in the lyrics. He also listens to Turkish music, especially arabesk and Turkish pop. Most important for him: break-dance. He is in a multi-background break dance crew, the Bionic B–Boys, who meet and practice at several youth centers, in the parks, and at the apartments of friends. – His friend Yu., neo-Muslim at least temporarily, has remarkable knowledge of a broad musical variety, including soul and rock. He knows the lyrics, tries to write himself, and is interested in media and movies (Interviews 2003).

Adolescents in open groups, such as Ke. and Yu., are often acquainted with many different forms of music also because the group members bring in their various favorite styles and songs. Language skills help them to understand the lyrics, and much additional information can be found on the internet. The groups enthusiastically practice dance moves and take the first steps in creating own productions. Through musical interests, people meet each other in their mobility throughout the city, and eventually cooperate with new friends. One favorite pastime is rapping, the rhythmical rhyming of lyrics.

Rap

There is an implicit feeling the park adolescents share about society[60] which is well-expressed in Tricia Rose's observation about rap in her study *Black Noise*: "Rap music … articulates the chasm between black urban lived experience and dominant, 'legitimate' (e.g., neoliberal) ideologies regarding equal opportunity and racial inequality" (Rose 1994:102). The author locates hiphop culture "within the context of deindustrialization" where inner-city youths' social roles are both reflected and contested (1994:22). Aidan Southall wrote, "Ghetto rap, blues, rock and dance have made their indispensable contribution to cultural self-worth and survival, apart from being, with Coca-Cola and hamburgers, the American city's most penetrating global export" (Southall 2000:393). In a more general way, popular cultures of oppressed groups have all the features Brian Ward finds in rhythm and blues: a critique of the system within the forms of the dominant culture (Ward 1998:4).

In black music, many park youths find they can identify with oppression, as this theme is featured at least as a sub-text. The currently most prominent form of black popular music is rap. Everybody in the parks is aware of rap, at least of the stereotype of gangster rap. To become a rapper is a, or even the, desired professional goal for many, and some groups have started rapping and rhyming:

> There is a page glued to the styrofoam sliding door which gives access to the sand-box press center: „Hände weg vom Bachapark" (hands off the Bacha-park), the title of a rap song written by park groups. The song has turned into the signation of the counter-garage squatter movement and is regularly performed at the winter and spring parties. Also, as by magic, other rap crews materialize in the park to participate in rap battles. – The park was squatted from January to June 2006, and the Bacherpark resistance movement against the subterranean garage victoriously disbanded when the poll they had demanded turned out against the garage.

"Rap, asserted Kurtis Blow at the time, is 'a way for the people of the ghetto to make themselves heard'", maintained popular music expert David Szatmary (1991:284) – a fact which park youth have not failed to notice, albeit in a vague and only partially reflected way. Park adolescents in Vienna could access this

---

60   I have elsewhere discussed black music's relevance and meaning for park groups (Mayer 2008).

Strictly Street Heroes # 4 (1998): Tupac Shakur

musical form due to rap's commercial mainstreaming since the 1990s. It is still a way to transport topics into wider circles and audiences, but it is only a few groups from parks – usually open groups – who forge and transpose their own experiences into rap songs[61].

Many park boys and girls are fans of the US mainstream rappers Tupac Shakur, Puff Daddy, Snoop Dogg, and 50 Cent; and the German rappers Bushido and Sido, who styled themselves after the US artists, have many followers in the Viennese parks. These rappers' lyrics and sounds are aggressive and often misogynist, and this style has been taken up with some success by Viennese rappers who were park-based, such as Sua Kaan, Stone Park, Nazar, and others. For them, their migration background is the main frame of reference. It is a mirror of what society calls them: "foreigners", or belonging to a "second" or "third generation". Against this dominant discourse, the artists plea either: "origins do not matter", or "I am the *real* Viennese", or the violent "get out of my

---

61   Zorica Rakic who did an in-depth study of Viennese active rappers says that, while these
     adolescents are as a group forced towards the peripheries of society (as migrants, as
     adolescents, as rappers), they want to take their place and position through rap with its
     global importance and local practices in adolescent scenes in Vienna (Rakic 2010:292).

Rappers Vlada and Ümit

park". Their success – with quick and critical media response to their violent lyrics and the musicians' public appearances on television – has encouraged the younger park boys' dreams of being rappers, and they know the lyrics by heart. But the step to creativity is not easy to take. The possibility of reflecting, verbalising, and acting out – a potentially political approach – remains only a daydream for many park boys, especially for those from closed cage groups.

German-speaking rappers' lyrics are more easily accessible to park groups than the US American originals, but there are other idols as well: rap is also produced in Istanbul, for example by famous and excessively quick-rapping Ceza, and his sister Ayben. Both are well known in Vienna, Ceza played a gig in a ball cage at Margaretengürtel in 2006[62] and at disco *Nachtwerk* in March 2009. Ayben played a rap gig in May 2009 in Ottakring. Both musicians' lyrics speak of Istanbul and present-day Turkey, of political topics, personal experiences and development. Ceza is widely known by Turkish-speaking and other park youth in Vienna, and has aroused much interest in rapping, rhyming, and writing lyrics among Viennese youngsters.

---

62   "Tuning the Cage" was part of *Into the City*, the street-styles-oriented productions of the high-culture festival *Wiener Festwochen*.

Aber mein größter Traum ist Rapper zu werden, das ist mein absoluter Traum. Ich bin schon auf dem Weg dahin. Ich und meine Band haben schon eigene CDs, wir gehen in Studios zum Proben, oder in den Park. Mein größtes Idol ist Ceza! (But my biggest dream is to become a rapper, this is my absolute dream. I am already on my way. Me and my band, we have our own CDs already, we go to studios to rehearse, or to the park. My biggest idol is Ceza!) (*Parkgeschichten* 2006:37).

Ceza is, however, not so much favored by many mainstream rap fans, who often find him too intellectual, whereas fans of Turkey-based musician Sagopa Kajmer, an older rapper with philosophical background, think that Ceza is shallow.

"They Don't Care About Us": Michael Jackson

Ring tone of a young boy's mobile phone at the Cash and Star internet café: Michael Jackson's "All I wanna say is that they don't really care about us". Some days later, a young kid enters Einsiedlerpark in the 5th District: his ring tone is Jackson's *Billie Jean* (August 2009).

Michael Jackson as a phenomenon was very important in the 1990s and he was enormously liked in the parks, voted as one of the street heroes by the park kids in 1997 (together with Muhammad Ali, Michael Jordan, Tupac Shakur, and Ronaldo). Much of his popularity was due to his dance style, especially for park groups with Roma background. Every park had one or more boys who called themselves "Jackson". His music and videos were the entry-ticket for many children into the world of global popular music – for example Ht. reminisces:

In the village in West Turkey, we all knew his songs, his impressive music videos, when we were still children at the end of the 1980s. He was the first big pop star for us, the first black person we knew, and we followed his transformations through the years (Conversation 2008).

And it seems Michael Jackson is still big in the parks today.

Arabesk

Anatolian arabesk is music played by a full orchestra, with very sad and pessimistic lyrics performed by an often flamboyant singer. In addition to mourning unrequited love, in the 1960s and 1970s the lyrics of arabesk songs expressed the people's political suffering from unjust social structures. Their subject matter were people's migration from rural (Eastern) Anatolia, the reasons they left the villages, and the ensuing processes of urbanization. Most families settled into the shantytowns around the big cities, the swelling gecekondus of Ankara and Istanbul. Quite a few arabesk movies were produced in Turkey, filmed in the gecekondus of Istanbul[63].

Famous arabesk artists include Ferdi Tayfur, Orhan Gencebay, Ibrahim Tatlises, and transvestite Bülent Ersoy. Listeners to Müslüm Gürses would often, as a ritual and ceremonial gesture, rip open their shirts and slash themselves with knives or razorblades, mostly across the chest or arms.

> I encountered this practice in the Flusser Park when I got to know Mr., a then 15 year-old park boy who showed us his scars after telling us that he was an ardent Müslüm fan (ca. 2002).

Arabesk came to Vienna on tapes and videocassettes brought or sent from Turkey. The contexts of migration, urbanization, and unjust social relations were not far from the people's experiences in Vienna. Arabesk was not youth music, but folk music shared by the old and young, expressing people's feelings and evoking faraway villages, towns, and cities. The lyrics are deep, often mystic, and oriented on Sufi poetry. Arabesk also sometimes involves drinking raki and other spirits, while listening to music and suffering from unreturned love, and the absence of women in general.

> "At school, we heard all the popular black stuff, Doctor Alban, MC Hammer … but in the park, only arabesk", says filmmaker Muzaffer Hasaltay of his park times in the 1990s (Conversation 2008).

Arabesk is a bit passé today in Viennese parks. The younger generation (those about 16 to 18 years old in 2010) are not as acquainted with arabesk as the park groups and their parents of the 1990s[64]. Today's versions and R'n Besk often lack any socio-political criticism, and mainly promote the new, urbanized, consumer-oriented globalized lifestyle of clothes, make-up, mobile phones, design, and furniture. In addition, aggressive US and German mainstream rap,

---

63 On arabesk, see also ethno-musicologist Martin Stokes (1992). On arabesk films, see Arslan: "*arabesk*, as the 'music of migration' belonged to urban peripheries, to shanty-towns that enacted a social existence in-between tradition and modernity" (2011:156).

64 Ethno-marketing aimed at Anatolian adults in Vienna makes use of these older arabesk songs, for example in cheese commercials on cable television programs.

Istanbul rapper Ceza, or Viennese rap artists have, with their straightforward lyrics of violence and frustration, replaced arabesk in the parks. However, rappers Sua Kaan play with arabesk, and use music samples in their newer productions (2010).

Dancing

The first wave of break dance in Vienna started around the time of movies like *Wild Style* and *Beat Street*. *Wild Style* (1982), the movie which was to have such a worldwide impact, was produced with very little money by New York artist Charlie Ahearn, who together with his team (with graffiti writers Lee Quinones and Sandra "Pink" Fabara, hiphop pioneers Grandmaster Flash, Busy Bee, The Cold Crush, and the Rock Steady Crew) brought the cracked concrete floors of the South Bronx ball play cages onto the silver screen.

In peripheral Vienna, in the large trans-Danubian housing projects such as especially the Großfeldsiedlung, first young breakers formed groups and met in battles in youth centers. This was in 1983 and 1984, and, as one dancer said then, "mia san olle Freind untereinanda", "we are all friends among each other" (*Die Wiener Break Dance Story,* 2010). The predominant dance style before the onset of b-boying and breaking was a Travolta-inspired disco dance.

Dancing was the dominant interest of many park kids in the 1990s. Most did an urban disco style (Michael Jackson dance), or followed the prominent singer and dancer Erdo, from the 5th District, and his freestyle acrobatic dance. Others started a renewed wave of breakdancing, and the linoleum on park floors was part and parcel of every party. Groups were Dynamic Skills and Resurrection, and the B-Boy Soul Tribe with DJ Zuzee (from the Großfeldsiedlung as well).

Dancing held options, and the best dancers – who became famous around Vienna from appearing at dance battles, and *Move Your Bones* gatherings (Vienna-wide dance competitions organised by the youth centers) – went on to compete on a Europe-wide dance battle scene. Becoming famous and adored was great for the adolescents and young men, and to impress the girls was a motivation as well. The competition of break dance and freestyle crews, and their gathering for the events, brought a Vienna-wide crowd into being. Already in 1984, one breaker said, we all know each other, there is no-one better or the boss (*Wiener Break Dance Story,* 2010). As people (mostly boys and young men) met each other, new formations were eventually founded.

Career options included working as a dance instructor, mainly in youth centers. Though some dancers had international success, the regional Viennese options were important for making money. Dancing in discotheques brought finan-

Singer and Dance-Star Erdo, Einsiedlerpark 1997

Breakers: Dynamic Souls at Check den Park (1997)

cial reward and publicity. However, none of the dancers – neither those from the peripheral housing projects, nor the inner-city park boys – had access to funds needed for establishing further business options, such as opening a professional dance studio, or producing larger entertainment productions. The boys remained dependent on the occasional sponsor, nightclubs, and money from youth work, and their own dance art was dependent on style fashions and trends in the global popular culture, therefore subjected to ups and downs, booms and crashes.

Their former young dance-days are often perceived as the best times ever by the former stars: they had first success, became famous, first money, first loves. An initiation of today, with breakdancing as dares and battle games as tests of courage, showing off, showing oneself in ever new ways, and doing gender in battling, competition, style, clothes. As Erdo says, "in the dance competitions, we wanted to proof ourselves, we wanted to be somebody" (*Wiener Break Dance Story*, 2010).

In Vienna's very city center, in front of the Stephansdom, a Hungarian break dance crew works since 12 years, attracting and influencing and also integrating Viennese adolescents who are especially fond of the crew's philosophy: that all people are equal. In recent break dance battles held in the large youth center *Ser Haus*, girls compete as well, and the participants, as a girl says in an interview, come from many places, from Russia like herself, from the Ukraine, from Hungary, Turkey, the former Eastern Block, the Yugoslavian follow-up states (*Wiener Break Dance Story*, 2010).

As an example of a crew's formation and development, the Bionic B-Boys' history gives a good glimpse from the inside (ca. 2002, German in original):

Bionic B-Boys History

We got infected with break dance fever by the videos of many break dance crews, such as the *Flying Steps* and also by the break dance workshop led by Rico from *Resurrection*. When the *Breakas in da Arena* started to break(dance), Twister, Lil Boy, and the others started as well. Wherever, however, whenever, we always practiced. We practiced in various youth centers, on basketball courts, wherever we could. In the meantime, Turbo and Sonic left the group. But they still met often and practiced together. In the year that Sonic and Turbo came to their new crew *Soulsonic Scills* (sic), Turbo gave up. Twister and Lil Boy then founded their own crew named *Magnetic B-Boys*. We decided with an old friend, Mikey, to found a group, and this crew still exists, the *Bionic B-Boys*. After some months, Sonic joined us. In the meantime Turbo from the former crew *Soulsonic Scills* joined us. Bionic B-Boys 4ever!

Bionic B-Boys: Turbo, Twister and Lil Boy

The Bionic B-Boys were based in the 5th District, mainly in the Seitstiegen Park, and disbanded a couple of years later, with members growing up and finding jobs, or having to attend the military service.

In the Viennese parks the break dance craze seems to have waned in recent years, at least concerning its active performance. Dancing in general is still part of girls' times in the park, they come together and study moves and choreographies in some remoter corner; sometimes copying music-clip inspired styles.

Older Park Kids: How Do You Feel?

Adolescents, as they grow up, become increasingly aware of their position in society – one of coming of age's main developmental tasks. Asking older adolescents how they felt often prompted frustrated answers. Some of them, however, did not go to the park any more, or not as regularly.

> Ae., 19, had a self-induced accident in which he hurt his leg badly after heavy drinking to celebrate the end of his service time in the army. It is not easy for him to come to terms with his failure, and he is on an extended sickness leave (6 months) from his much-liked job as a builder. "How are you?"
> – „Nicht so super, das Arbeiten geht mir ab, alle Freunde arbeiten. Ich lasse alles auf mich zukommen, schlafe bis die Freunde anrufen." ("Not so good. I miss work, all my friends work. I let everything come to me, sleep until my

friends call me") – sometimes until the afternoon. He thinks that fate defines life. It can be a little, but not much, altered, and „alles hängt mit allem zusammen", "everything is connected with everything else". He often thinks, "scho wieder so a Scheißtag", "another fucking day". He hopes that everything will turn out well again, "Hoffnung ist das wichtigste, ohne Hoffnung ist man verloren", hope is the most important thing, and without hope one is lost. – Ae. was a regular in the Flusser Park when he was younger, sometimes together with his elder brother Ch. They also hung out in the small green next to where they lived, the social housing complex at the Wolkenkratzer Park, and often went to the nearby youth center. Both brothers, however, were not very deeply integrated into any park group. (Interview 2005).

Ae. was very much in accord with the Austrian working-class life in the well-paid and highly prestigious building trade. The military service was consistent with this social goal, and he had his contacts there as well, presumably the same friends of his age-set with whom he had worked with before and, he hoped, would be working with afterwards, and this hope seemed to come true. With the at least temporary interruption of this plan, life lost its meaning for him. Life without work was clearly empty, and he could not fill the time with any productive alternative. His social and emotional network were congruent, and, although his friends did not drift away from him and his contacts with them were still strong, even daily, their shared interests had gradually decreased. Ae. had to make ends meet, as his peers all now have an enormous financial advantage over him: he cannot keep up his former lifestyle. Although Ae. had still more money at hand than the other interviewees, he was the unhappiest among them.

For Ae., military service was not an interruption in his life, with the continuation of friendships from work. For other young men, the still obligatory Austrian military service[65] is something like a welcome recess from job-seeking. Many were having a hard time finding an apprenticeship or a job, were constantly without money, had useless time on their hands, were pressured by parents, and by the "trash subjectivity" (Rolnik 2006) connected to their "failure". While the time in service often disrupts the park peer groups at least temporarily, there are also new friends to be made in the army.

---

65 There is the option of doing a social year instead. The general military service is currently in political debate.

Ke., 19, in the army at time of the interview. "How do you feel?" – „Ja, eh gut, jetzt hab ich Freunde beim Heer. Aber ich hätt es mir anders vorgestellt, mit Führerschein machen und so, es ist alles schiefgelaufen. Aber Hauptschule war super." ("Ok, now that I have friends in the army. But I imagined this differently, with a driving license, but everything went wrong. But school was super"). (2005).

In the unstructured times after school and before the military service, going to the park and meeting his closely-knit Seitstiegen Park friendship group was essential for Ke. After difficult post-school times – he sent out at least one hundred applications for an apprenticeship – the military service has brought regularity into his life, which he, after finding friends, now enjoys.

Another young man from the Seitstiegen Park group, Su., had other difficulties to overcome:

Su. just turned 20. He now lives in a student-home, sharing his room with one boy. In the evenings he works as a cocktail mixer in a bar. Su. does not have Austrian citizenship yet; he came to Austria from Sri Lanka, with his father, when he was twelve. Su. and his father got into financial trouble: they lost their apartment, found another one, lost it again. Father and son then separated, each trying to make ends meet on his own. Su. moved in with friends, several youths from Sri Lanka, for some months, but this deeply depressed him. They did not have enough room, and could not really accommodate him; so he always carried a bag with clothes and his documents with him in case he found somewhere else to spend the night. He felt humiliated and hopeless. But now, in the student home, it is much better. He says he has been down, all the way to the bottom. One of his biggest problems now is his lack of citizenship, without which he must fear for his residence permit in Austria, and also cannot get better jobs. Su. is from the Seitstiegen group, but they could not help him in his homelessness as they are all living with their parents. But still, Su.'s park-based friendships persisted (Interview 2005).

Such homelessness does not very frequently occur, although some youths leave their homes to stay with friends for a certain time. Su.'s difficulties stemmed from his father's – who was in difficult circumstances himself, often ill, frequently unemployed – and from lacking citizenship, which causes constant worry, documents expenses, and limited opportunities for work or welfare support; and any work he can get is likely to be low-paying.

But his open park group was still a good support, and their common interests – break dance, hiphop, music in general – were a creative outlet which also provides a positive self-image, a "performing subjectivity".

Others, either alone or in groups, cannot fall back on positive group images, and don't pursue meaningful activities.

> We meet Za. again, who turned twenty already. He is on his own in the ball cage of Hofpark, shooting some baskets. He is bored and unhappy. We had not seen him for a long time, he was a Flusser Park and Hofpark regular years ago and moved on, took up work. What happened? He lost his job, cannot find another, comes to the park because he cannot stand being at home all the time – he hopes to meet someone from the old days in the park.

Za. feels that he should not hang out in the park any more, and if he does, it will show that he's a loser, and he also has this impression of himself. But alternative meeting places are not established. So by going to the park he hopes to meet friends from the old days, and maybe others are in the same situation as he is. For him and those like him, parks have changed from positive places for sports and fun into increasingly negative places, *heterotope* spaces where his disconnection from society is palpable.

Under-Demand and Regularity

In some respects, the free park life is very social and fun, with a diverting variety of experiences. When people are still young, growing from children into adolescents, it is cool to move into the park's social structures with their greater freedom. This is also a period when economic standing is yet unimportant, expenses are easily shared among kids in a group, and the few desires are inexpensive. The park can be an enjoyable after-school and after-work hangout, a meeting place to come together with friends, and to get to know new people. But growing up without money makes the hard facts of exclusion increasingly tangible. A division within and among park groups becomes noticeable. For the economically excluded, the park life turns sour: too many wishes and desires, and too little money; too much time, and nothing to fill it with.

Their lack of success, at least in economic terms, causes older adolescents to become acutely aware of their exclusion from consumption-dominated urban life. Some seek explanations in their own inadequacy, and self-blame and frustration follow. Others feel that society is unjust, and blame capitalism, racism, or politicians who do nothing to help them out. Whole groups fall into the black hole of unemployment and feelings of uselessness. The hours in the park can become very long: after a soccer game and some chatting and horseplay, time begins to stretch out interminably.

These problems are rarely solved in park life with the peers, as chronic under-demand will take its toll on youth's spirits and self-view. Therefore, creative solutions, or creativity as a solution, are not taken up by those who are most deprived. Rapping and break dance or other youth-cultural styles and expressions are more likely to be chosen by youth groups who are better off, who have some kind of support and back-up, and who are inclined to follow their interests. But for many groups in under-demand conditions, clearly defined interests and political positions are not developed beyond mere wishful thinking and dreams about money.

> The work structure defines the weekly structure. Those young people who work in Monday-to-Friday morning-to-evening day jobs or spend their days in military service rather liked the weekends and made a clear distinction between workdays and weekend regarding their daily routines and different activities. Those unemployed and/or on sick leave did not make this distinction, and did not speak of special weekend activities. Nobody mentioned family activities on weekends. Only Ae. said that he avoided home on weekends because his mother was home then, which stressed him (Interviews 2005).

The classic work routine has become generally out-moded, and for an increasing part of the urban population the norm is an unstructured work schedule with few differences between weekdays and weekends, night and day. Moreover and increasingly, both unemployment and over-employment (that is extra-long working hours, and the extra time involved e.g. in running a small neighborhood grocery or mobile phone shop) have further fractured family routines.

For many adolescents, regularity is an unknown quality of life. Dropping out of school, and frequent truancy, also aggravate already irregular lives. Even if one attends school until 15, school usually ends at noon, and school children and young people are on their own. Park kids go to the park, and daily routines might be dominated by weather, soccer game results, the park groups' emotional state, the availability of money and, for some, drugs. But if adolescents are given regulated time structures, they adapt easily and willingly.

Sf. enjoys the strict structures of sports. He began playing soccer in a club a short time ago. – Su. sometimes felt like a grown-up vis-à-vis his father, with the father sometimes acting like an unruly child. He feels better since living on his own (in a students' home) where he built up, and is now able to follow, his own routines. – Ke. praises the regular meals in the military service, and the getting up early does not bother him, although it was hard in the beginning. – De. says that as a lazy[66] person, she needs a schedule and structures.

If a young person from a park background comes into structured circumstances which roughly fit his or her previous positive experiences – being together with peers or new friends in a supportive atmosphere – or which correspond to their expectations of a good life (like playing soccer in a club), then a park youth can and will accommodate to the new situation, and even strict structures are welcome and experienced as positive, for example the regular meals in the military service mentioned by Ke.

This positive response to regularity is a symptom of the chronic under-demand the adolescents face in their park lives. The self-structured under-demand of such park groups quickly becomes the unsatisfying norm. Park time is rarely perceived as holding a potential for productivity, as time usefully spent, which furthers one's development. They find long-term planning impossible; and outside attempts at structuring their lives are not welcome if not in accordance with their own movements and at their own pace.

---

66   See also Digruber's in-depth study of second generation girls' job experiences, they often spoke of themselves as "lazy" (2003:111).

2. Spatial and Social Contexts

The park peer groups are the adolescents' most important social contacts, and the parks and cages are their meeting places, their basic points of reference, topographically and socially. But in growing up they also venture out of the park and explore the surroundings and common urban areas, and their radius of experience and activities – including employment and jobs across the city – widens.

a. Park Neighborhoods

Apart from the public spaces around the parks there are indoor places in the neighborhood which are important to park youth. These are commercial, such as betting shops and gambling arcades, certain internet cafés, coffeehouses; or institutional, such as the youth centers, and sometimes meeting rooms of churches, mosques, and private associations. Generally, institutional rooms are for the younger adolescents. With growing age, they find institutional rooms are too regulated, and swing to commercial places as these become more accessible to them.

Youth Centers and Rooms for Adolescents

Vienna is a city with a long-standing welfare tradition. The municipality offers much support to adolescents, and local youth centers are a major social and leisure resource for park kids. Depending on the groups and their conduct, they attend regularly or only sporadically. Some park boys from closed groups might not muster the social skills necessary for the youth centers, but they probably attended earlier, as children, and are usually quite well acquainted with the local center and the people working there.

The most important events for younger adolescents are the weekly disco evenings in youth centers. Older adolescents drop by regularly as part of their evolving clubbing and party activities, or show up occasionally. Some are DJs and enjoy being admired by the younger kids.

Youth centers also offer a youth café with games, training space for break dance, equipment for producing music and rap, and video studios. Rooms in general are a scarce resource for park groups, and they are in constant need of going somewhere indoors, as the parks do not offer much shelter, and apart from playing soccer, there is not much to do.

Other room options in the neighborhood exist on the premises of confessional religious groups as part of their youth work. Neighborhood mosques often have such open rooms for adolescents.

> A narrow staircase leads down to where the mosque youth room is: it is not very large, walls and carpeted floors are a drab brown. There are some leisure time activities (games, cards); cheap soda and soft drinks and tea are available. There is one elderly man in charge who does not seem very interested. There are some girls and boys who play cards, and the atmosphere is quiet and relaxed.

Generally, apart from cold winter days, the mosque rooms are not very attractive to the kids. Some boy groups say that they go to the mosque to play cards, and they also attend the Friday prayers, and just hang out. Increasing religious involvement sometimes takes an adolescent away from the park, and he might try to influence his peers to do likewise. But more often, unruly park groups get tired of the strict mosque rules and stop going there.

> A Catholic Church had a cool party location in a basement in the 5th District, a large club hall with several adjacent smaller rooms. Adolescents' use of the premises was almost uncontrolled, and some hot parties went down, organized by the park groups themselves who also had the keys. After some months, however, the person in charge was transferred, and the location's party times were over (1997).

Institutional rooms such as this one serve a variety of developmental processes because they enable contact and interaction with other adolescents, adolescent groups, and grown-ups in a partially supervised setting, suitable for trying out different roles while growing up.

But there are still long hours when youth centers and other rooms are not available – so back to the park. If the park groups are able to muster sufficient financial resources, commercial places in the neighborhood become an extension of park life. These places are local coffee shops and certain internet cafés, but increasingly also betting shops and gambling arcades. All these places must be compatible with youth demands, and there are many where, for some reason, they are not welcome, or which are not attractive to young people due to their restrictions. Usually only a small number of places in the park neighborhoods are possible retreats for the groups.

Large shopping malls are important commercial hang-outs for adolescents, and usually attract youth from other districts as well. Thus malls are part of the "common urban places" rather than neighborhood places. "Mall kids" are a special phenomenon of growing up in cities[67].

Commercial Neighborhood Places
Win Or Lose ...

> I'm in the 5th District at a kebab and börek house run by a man from the kara deniz area. I meet Oe., now 17, from the former Eremit Park, then Flusser Park group. He tells me that he is in funded training to be a plumber. His twin brother Me. will become a bricklayer. – After finishing his dürüm, he crosses the street and enters the betting café on the corner. Later that evening I see On., 19 years old, one of their group, enter as well. – Two months later at the same place, I see Oe., his brother Me., and their friend Vl. coming out of the same betting place (Summer 2009).

These encounters and observations show that Oe., Me., On., and Vl. – "the old gang", a closed soccer cage group – are still doing things together; that they successfully got into funded job training and therefore have some money; and that they have taken to frequenting betting shops.

Betting and gambling shops and game arcades are almost exclusively patronized by male customers. The places are open to people from age 18, but the law is not strictly enforced. Consequently, a number of park adolescents have begun to go to these places regularly. Youth worker Andrea Schmidt (2006) observed this to be the case especially for Turkish/Anatolian boys. Not a few young men have debts resulting from losing at betting and slot machines. The *JugendZone 16*, youth center in Vienna's 16th District, reports similar results in their Sozialraumstudie (study of social space, 2000): betting, as Christian

---

67   See Norbert Gestring and Ute Neumann „Von Mall Rats und Mall Bunnies. Jugendliche in Shopping Malls", in: Wehrheim, Jan (ed.) (2007), Shopping Malls. Interdisziplinäre Betrachtungen eines neuen Raumtyps. Pp. 135 – 152.

Holzhacker, manager of the youth center, states, becomes an adolescent's important vehicle for establishing self-worth, the pull-factors are considerable, and the amount of money lost is frightening[68].

Neighborhood Cafés

A neighborhood option for adolescents are cafés maintained by people with the group's, or one of the group's, vernacular, often owned by a relative. Some of these places attract mainly young people, but others are multi-generational. Betting and gambling machines increasingly dominate such neighborhood cafés, and the distinction between betting/gambling places and cafés has begun to dissolve.

Boys and young men with Anatolian background go to the Kaffeehaus. Places are favored that are close to the relevant parks. The Anatolian café is a male-dominated neighborhood institution and can be seen as a commercial living room where men come together to spend their leisure time. There are

---

68   Cited in Gedlicka Karl, "Zwischen Park und Wettcafé", Der Standard, May 16th, 2010, available online http://derstandard.at/1271376645107/Jugendliche-in-Ottakring-Zwischen-Park-und-Wettcafe.

newspapers, games, and playing cards. Two or more large television screens dominate the room, offering music videos, news, football, and commercials from Turkish cable stations.

Adolescent boys start going to the Kaffeehaus from around 14 or 15 years of age. They have a certain shyness at first, and go with an older or more experienced boy, or in groups. They play cards, and drink tea or sometimes beer. They avoid their fathers and older relatives, who in turn pretend not to see them. The young park groups will frequent several coffee houses, eventually choosing one as a major meeting place.

An Anatolian café usually has a strong political and/or religious background reflecting the owner's views, expressed by the choice of newspapers and advertisements (posters, concert announcements, leaflets and flyers) available in the establishment. In the coffee house, pairs or groups of young park boys grow into a larger social network through contact with the older men, experimenting with new roles. Coffeehouses are an important arena for their, as Hannerz would call it, "growing up male" (2004:118ff.).

Internet Cafés

The internet cafés are important focal points in the neighborhood grid and provide the park youth with affordable access to virtual realities and the world wide web. Increasingly many working-class households have cheap computers and also internet access, but there are still many who do not. In some households with access, the data transfer rate is very slow, or the amount paid for is too quickly used up. The technical devices might often be out of order or broken, and repair is impossible or too costly: instead, a new set will be bought at the next opportunity. But park adolescents probably prefer to go with their peers to the internet café anyway.

Internet cafés have opened at every corner in the old working-class district neighborhoods and along the Gürtel. Some of these places can be termed park youth places, virtually crawling with young people at times. Access is not restricted; there is almost no control; communication and games are cheap. Because of this atmosphere, few adult users are there: they frequent other places.

Many internet cafés close late. They are firmly rooted in neighborhood surroundings and are often family-run businesses. Many of the shops also have telephone booths, and the special rates (to Turkey, Africa, the Middle or Far East, Arab countries) reflect owners' and customers' backgrounds and communication needs.

Some neighborhood internet cafés, especially where it is possible to play interactive computer games such as Counter Strike, are almost exclusively frequented by boys:

> Ich komme am Nachmittag in den Park und ich treffe mich mit meinen Freunden und dann gehen wir Counter Strike spielen. (I come to the park in the afternoon, meet my friends, and then we go to play Counter Strike.) (*Parkgeschichten* 2006:15).

Counter Strike has been the most popular interactive computer game. It can be played by up to 8 players who assemble in the internet café.

> 9 p.m. at the Money and Moon in a poorer high street in the 18th District. There are around 10 younger boys. Most do not have broken voices yet; one cannot be older than 7 years, and there are some young adults in the back room. All are playing CS. With much mutual support and a lot of discussions, they get involved in the game quite quickly. „Welchen Namen nimmst du?" ("What do you call yourself?") – „Die sind fast tot" ("They're almost dead".) – „Warte, ich mach mehr Spieler" ("Wait, I make more players") – „Wir verlieren eh" ("We'll lose anyway") – "Wie hast du gemacht?" ("How did you do [that]?") – „Wo bist du heast?" ("Where are you, listen?") – „Was machst du dort Oida?" ("What are you doing there old chap?") (Communication in German, August 2009).

The design of Counter Strike shows run-down post-urban surroundings: grey concrete walls, partially overgrown industrial complexes, and derelict military bases, garages, and hangars. The game is about terrorists and an anti-terrorists police unit, and the walls bear graffiti in Arabic script.

> The player moves behind his gun. „He, jetzt hast du mich erschossen, du Idiot!" ("Hey, now you shot me dead, you idiot!") (Money and Moon, August 2009).

Interactive digital games can be understood as an imagined version of "real" war[69].

> I meet Ys., 17, in the restricted-access back-room of an internet café in the
> 5th District; while the others are playing interactive games outside, he sits
> smoking and downloading US-American gangsta rap music clips – he ma-
> nages this despite his illiteracy. He likes the weapons, the violence, the cool
> attire. In fact, this is not much different from his own life. His violence has
> already gotten him into jail several times (July 2007).

For Ys., the time in front of the computer screen is a break from his otherwise
violence-dominated life as he can sit inside with a cigarette, protected, and off
the street. Outside, any time another troublesome incident could come up. On
the other hand, the globally connected computer world is the extended version
of his street life, as he seeks out virtual experiences that duplicate his street life
outside in new images.

---

69 See also Peggy Trawick's contribution on "Cyberkids in Metropolitan America" (2007).
    She cites the posting of one Total Annihilation game addict as follows: "Can't we fight
    real world wars on computer games? ... Less bloody, same concept." (2007:210).

The internet has become the main source of information for park adolescents in general. News is sought on stars and starlets, music and musicians, on sex, and war. Via the interactive options of the worldwide web, the "old" or "classical" media (newspapers and TV) are by-passed and the kids contribute their own posts, making themselves globally visible and accessible to communication. Pictures/images and videos are particularly looked for.

Many park-based adolescents are insecure in their practices of knowledge and not firm at reading and writing, and therefore cannot, and do not, make much use of text-based information in this huge global memory and history storage system. For those still at school, the internet is a difficult source for finding useful information for their home-works and school projects, although teachers try to train pupils in competent net use.

Those already in their post-school days (whether prematurely or by graduation) are not encouraged to hone their reading and writing skills; so their desiderata from the net are music and images. The videos currently most often sought out and watched by park adolescents are those of spectacular accidents, followed by music clips and their do-it-yourself re-makes, videos of fights and other violent incidents (often in former homelands[70]), curiosities of all sorts, and pornography.

On you-tube, the view count and the "most watched videos" section guide users; the comments are interesting to get in touch with like-minded people. Even with weak reading and writing skills, it is possible to enter a worldwide scene, often in the adolescents' own vernaculars.

Girls and boys frequent chat rooms, and sometimes, after exchanging mobile phone numbers, the boy and girl meet face to face. Usually the adolescents surf together with their peers, and the experimenting with new adult roles and with sexuality is experienced from a supported position.

Instant messenger systems are important for the Vienna-wide exchange among adolescents, used daily and sometimes hourly to arrange meetings and to contact friends and family, and increasingly many youths are on myspace. com and on Facebook.

E-Bay is used predominantly for checking out cars and motorcycles. Also popular is the download of screen savers and screen backgrounds, often national symbols and flags, but also musicians. Many adolescents who frequent clubs and discos download pictures from clubbings (at Volksgarten, Nacht-

---

70   For example, videos of Chechen Mudjaheddin are very prominent among male adolescent refugees from the Caucasus regions.

werk, Nachtschicht, etc.). Another use is the internet telephone function, with or without camera, for communicating with friends, and also with relatives abroad.

Access to virtual rooms and spaces provides opportunities for meeting people, and for sharing experiences and knowledge. This partially compensates for the general lack of physical space (both at home and in the urban surroundings) and social space (in society as such, including political participation). Virtual reality opens up new playgrounds of identity and specific imagined realities. E-Bay has turned into such a space as well: consumer fantasies of mobility are lived out – such as having a car of one's own.

Virtual communication of any sort strengthens the interaction among peers, friends, and relatives. The activities on and around the net are, from my observations of the park adolescents in question, peer group activities. Whether playing Counter Strike, or looking up gangsta rap lyrics, or watching weird accidents on You-Tube, or going to a flirt chat room – all these activities involve the group who are watching, playing, communicating.

Cage group members were usually headed for meeting their groups and peers in the parks to play soccer, but they increasingly often went to internet cafés while this study lasted. Other park groups spent more time at home, probably with a computer; and older adolescents and young adults who had already left their park times behind were connected to the web at home. So the trend towards individualised home access to the internet is surely spreading, and probably one general trend also for park adolescents and young adults in Viennese society is towards more isolated time spent at home alone in front of the PC. This might coincide with, and stimulate, the retreat from parks as main spaces of group activity.

Television

> At Cs.'s home the TV is constantly turned on in the living room. His mother likes to watch the market programs: and indeed, it is not bad, the host encouraging people to estimate how many kilograms of oranges are in a bag. A little game for customers and market stall employees! Next: a commercial for a bridal shop. It is a Turkish program produced in Vienna and broadcast via cable television (May 2009).

Most homes have television sets, which dominate entertainment and socializing. Parental TV use often includes satellite programs from, about, or in the languages of former homelands. Commercials and entertainment programs broadcast in and from Vienna are targeted at ethno-marketing[71] which, on satellite and cable TV, includes advertisements for textile and grocery shops, market and fast food stalls, restaurants, and locations for (life-cycle) family celebrations. The images and music used in these ads aim directly at the "target" groups' immigrant backgrounds and exploit memories of their youth and homelands.

It is not uncommon for young people and even children to have television sets in their rooms. Household budgets might be stressed to the limit and beyond, but ubiquitous supply with cheap technical equipment and infotainment is part and parcel of many consumer-oriented working-class homes[72]. Game consoles are very popular, and some park boys grow up with it and go on playing far into adulthood[73].

Community TV and Park TV

> Park TV interview. Q: „Wie lange bist du schon hier in diesem Park?" – A: „Seit ich mich kenne!" ("How long have you been in this park?" – "Since I know myself!") (Park TV, May 2009).

In Vienna, participatory community television Okto[74] invites, supports, and distributes "do-it-yourself" television. Programs by and for young people have been an important and integral part from the start. Presently, such broadcasts include Park TV, CU Television, and several other productions.

Park-based adolescents from various districts produce low-key, youth work-supported Park TV. This format grew out of media youth projects with park children and adolescents from 2002 on. Groups organised discussions in their park that were recorded on video and then showed in a park in another district, where they again stimulated new discussions. In course of this project, youth groups used the video cameras to record their own stories[75]. Sub-

---

71 Personal information by Onur Serdar.
72 Enunciation without comparable data from middle class and elite homes and families. See also Mutsch (2008).
73 Play Station, e.g., is prominent in the lives of the young men in Hasaltay's short movie *Der Freund*.
74 See www.okto.tv, and the booklet 5. *Eine Foto Love Story. Wir machen Fernsehen.* Okto Community TV (ed.), 2010. Okto is largely supported by the municipality.
75 The collected material was edited into a feature film presented at the *Park TV Gala* in the Millennium City, a shopping center in the 20th District and a magnet for adolescent groups from all around town. The event was celebrated with a grand party in the cinema foyer, which attracted around 500 young visitors.

CU Television team: Matthias Buchensteiner, Richi Kuong, Georg Rudolf, Sebastian Mair, Konstantin Pepaj, Lorenco Stevanovic, Pedro Diaz-Figueroa (back row); Petra Saßmann, Ludowika Grindl, Nasrin Qasimi, Luminita Damaschin, Julietta Bangiew, Diana-Carolina El Masri, Mileva Kadiqi, Susann Abad (front row)

sequently, the format of Park TV was carried on as a cooperative effort of park adolescents and youth work in the 16th, 17th and 20th District.

CU Television, a production of the Verein Wiener Jugendzentren, has a growing team of young journalists, moderators, and reporters. They edit own productions and numerous video contributions by the more than 30 youth centers and mobile youth work teams in Vienna.

Countless adolescents and groups from districts, parks, and youth centers all around the city have been, and continue to be, featured on Park TV and on CU Television in their monthly programs. It is a mediated version of adolescents' and also park life, a youth- and neighborhood television where personal acquaintances, park friends, cousins, or oneself appear on screen. The viewers and the viewed form an integrated public, and television has become accessible, approachable, and manageable, a gossip medium on a Vienna-wide scale.

b. The City at Large: Common Urban Space

The park groups feel comfortable in their neighborhoods, but around them is the city at-large. Some might not need to go into the common urban space, and some would rather stay put in the parks and cages. Some subsequently frequent parks and common urban space; others by and by leave the parks entirely, and integrate into the larger urban crowds. This enlarging of one's radius of action and knowledge is part of growing up, and also connected to the beginning of job and work experiences which may lead a youth far away from his or her home neighborhood into new, and often not very welcoming, surroundings.

Some urban youth meeting places have a long history – for example Reumannplatz in the 10th District, a focus for park-based adolescents mainly from Favoriten and the adjacent Margareten, where a hundred kids and more often meet. New urban group meeting places are being established in malls, Cineplex centers, and such attractive central shopping high streets as the Mariahilfer Strasse, where numerous adolescents stroll up and down in groups and pairs. In summer, kids also frequent outdoor swimming pools (the park groups from the 5th District went to the Laaberg Bad of the 10th, and the Simmeringer Bad of the 11th District), the Donauinsel with the Copa Cagrana (a youth-affine consumer zone along the Danube River with numerous clubs and cafés); and the Prater amusement park.

Shopping Malls

Places belonging to the adolescents' world, and therefore favored by park-based and park-socialized adolescents, are malls and the included multiplex cinemas, mainly those – Millennium City, Lugner City, Donauzentrum, and Gasometer – which are situated in working-class areas.

> The Seitstiegen group has celebrated! Somebody's birthday came up, and they all went to one of the restaurants in the Lugner City. It was quite cool, as Ja. told me; it was his idea, because he is in vocational training in one of the mall's clothing stores. They all liked it a lot and will probably go again sometime. A good atmosphere was offered, and they found the prices to be adequate: not cheap, but not expensive either (Conversation 2005).

For the open Seitstiegen Park group with their growing experiences in urban space and commercial places, there were no problems encountered in using the shopping center as a leisure time facility. These malls employ numerous secu-

rity personnel in charge of monitoring the visitors and consumers. Poor youth groups are quick to see the excluding signs aimed at keeping them out. Others try to observe the rules, and enjoy the integrated cinema centers, the associated betting and gambling halls, video parlors, lounges, restaurants, fast food places, and cafés, which supply the adolescents with a full leisure-time concept without the necessity of stepping out into cold weather, traffic, and boring streets.

Consumers are, in these working-class area malls, to a substantial part of immigrant background. Children are introduced to various festival traditions, which are enacted as colorful simulacra in the atrium of the building. Stairways and balconies serve as spectator stands for the merry activities; non-commercial spaces to sit and interact are sparse. The mall provides 'security' – not safety – for all: shoppers, dealers, entertainers, and entrepreneurs. If adolescents are willing and able to grow into these disciplined, controlled, and normed consumer structures, they are welcome and also enjoy the ambivalent blessings of a guarded space (against enemy groups and other troubles); if not, and if goals other than consuming are on their minds, they are quickly thrown out, and they are banned from sharing in the shopping centers' new forms of sociability: the staged in-door merging of experience and adventure with consumption.

Clubs and Discos

For many park adolescents, the coming of age also includes initiation into the clubbing and disco scenes.

> Ae. sleeps long everyday, often until midday or afternoon. His mother is away at work until the evening, when he goes out to dance at clubs. He started to frequent alternative clubs, likes reggae and ragga, and developed a critical worldview. After his accident, he made new friends: students, politically active people.

> The older Katzenpark groups very often meet in the evenings and at night at the park, before going out to clubs. Se., a well-liked chap among his peers in the Katzenpark who he mainly hangs out with, spends all his leisure time there with them and with his girlfriend. He gets up at 6 and goes to work, and on weekends he sleeps till noon, then heads down to the park to meet his friends. Friday and Saturday evening they all go to large clubs like the Nachtwerk, or to the Copa Cagrana on the Danube.

Some adolescents begin clubbing on their own, but most start going to clubs with their park group. We already met Ae. and Se.: both were quite frustrated with their lives and how everything turned out. Clubbing became important for them and provided new spirits, and Ae. made new friends and eventually found out of his crisis.

Many of the younger kids have their first experiences of sex and drugs in clubs. Their lives can change dramatically in a single evening by romance found or lost, by a first experience with drugs, by fights, or by new friends or enemies.

> The cellar-club in the 2nd District had its youth clubbing on Friday evenings and Sunday afternoons. Many groups from the 5th District went regularly, when DJ Dv. played there – he was also a DJ at the youth center and had a huge following. His girlfriend, aged 13, went to every clubbing with him. There were very young kids as well, 9 or 10 years old. Older guys acted as security guards because there were a lot of fights, some involving knives; especially outside with people who had been denied entrance, or who were thrown out (observations from 1997 to 2001, memories by Le., 2007).

Clubs where young people go to are in constant change, closing, re-opening, going in and out of fashion. Clubs are either mixed, basically open to all who "know how to behave" (indicated also by outfit and style), or "closed" in the sense of

having racist club policies ("whites only"). Some clubs are frequented by certain minority groups and are hubs for information, exchange, and social life.

> One night out at the Nachtwerk: we make the rounds on the huge, flood-lighted parking lot, showing off our ancient yolk-yellow Ford Granada. Hey, there's Dm., aged 16, from the 20th District, with a girl on each arm! He notices us – the car! –, and acknowledges us with a wink. He passes the huge bouncers at the entrance gates, and vanishes inside. We follow into the enormous cylindrical hall, which is surrounded by several balconies where one can look down onto the dance floor and the elevated DJ fittings. Numerous golden cages are scattered around the dance floor, the dancers inside moving smoothly. Later, in a separate small café down the hall, people dance *kolo* (a line dance) while women strip in booths along the walls. A special feature is the famous Geldregen (money shower) in the huge disco: real bills rain down on the dancers (1999).

The Nachtwerk, which is very far away from the city center, frequently hosts international live acts and concerts by artists from South-Eastern Europe and Turkey. Other places and club nights which cater to transnational and global musical tastes (Bodrum Nights, oriental parties, Balkan Fever, Balkan nights, the Club Ost, R'n' Besk clubbings, etc.) are organized by people with immigration backgrounds, and develop into increasingly popular open urban spaces.

Access to clubs is often denied to less refined urban adolescents who are quickly "ethnicized" by club owners and their security door guards. Experiences with violent groups, but also outright discrimination are the reasons for the selection. Many male teenagers' court appearances and jail sentences are the result of violent encounters in or outside clubs.

> We attend the group trial of five refugee adolescents. They started a huge
> fight outside a club in Vienna's First District during a New Years Eve party,
> when they tried to rob groups of clubbers. Only a few of the victims showed
> up at the trial. Others are called in vain, and we recognize the names: some
> park kids whom we know – in fact, kids from the Seitstiegen group, who had
> mentioned the incident to us (June 2007).

Closed groups, denied admission to the more exclusive clubs, react with what they know: violent physical behavior, returning for revenge to the place from which they had been rejected. But eventually, they tend to stay closer to "home" – stay local, in their home districts, in their neighborhood park and cage. Other groups (incipient gangs) move on in search of new opportunities, and expand their range of operations to other common urban spaces.

Many park youth frequent less posh places such as the cheaper clubs in working-class neighborhoods on Favoritenstrasse, Ottakringer Strasse, Märzstrasse etc. In these, often smaller, spots the rules of conduct are less strict than in the centrally located clubs, and they have a tougher public.

Clubs and discos are important places for initiations: fragmented and self-initiations, evolving from contact and, for some, conflict with adults (club owners, other visitors, bouncers, waiters and waitresses, musicians). Clubs hold a lot more options for experimenting with one's role than the parks. Experiences of exclusion are confirmed for the closed park groups; the open groups move on in their development as part of the urban crowd and scenes, with their distinct leisure-time lifestyles.

Favored Youth Places

> It is hottest July; Me.'s arm is in a plaster cast. How did this happen? He had a
> violent encounter with someone in the Laaberg Bad, an open-air swimming
> pool in the 10th District (2007).

Impression from disco Nachtschicht, 1997

Certain outdoor swimming pools, usually those with cheap entrance fees and not much "security", are working-class youth places. There, closed groups from different backgrounds and districts come into, often violent, contact.

A largely uncontrolled area where closed groups often go, especially if on truancy or after being (temporarily) expelled from school, is the Prater. This huge park with its associated carnival grounds offers practically unlimited recreational opportunity, but also holds chances for violent encounters with other groups, and for illegal activities.

To conclude, learning the ways of the city is part of growing up in urban surroundings. For open park groups this consists mainly in getting to know the urban retail areas and consumption spaces, and the clubs and discos. The expansion of a kid's personal radius sometimes begins when the youth is only 9 or 10 years of age. Closed groups, if they leave their soccer cage at all, are likely to get into trouble, such as expulsion from places and violent encounters, and are more attracted to uncontrolled areas. Others start pursuing illegal activities in the common urban spaces.

c. Work, Jobs, Wage Labor

General Situation

A weaker economy and changing political circumstances – from welfare politics to neoliberal economic strategies – strongly affect especially the park adolescents because they are vulnerable in terms of education, class background, family support, social skills, and language.

For the park youth, the financial resources to join in the consumer society is rarely provided by the parents and comes mainly from their own money, and increasingly often a whole family is un- or underemployed. Adolescents thus react under pressure and accept the first work that is on offer, however precarious.

> Talking about their jobs and work was not easy since a lot of frustration is to be found there. Either people were lucky to find a job at last – after long months of exhausting search – or they somehow lost a job they liked, which they regret; or they are still looking for one but don't really know how it will turn out. Somehow or other, they all know that they are in a very precarious situation, and that failure in that respect threatens them and their present life, as well as the future life, which seems increasingly uncontrollable. (Resume from the interviews 2005.)

Adolescents I have known have found jobs in the city services:

> On the subway. The driver announces my stop: Pilgramgasse. Something in his voice seems familiar. I get out and look into the driver's compartment: it is Hassan who was, as a pupil, in our intercultural training class in a Hauptschule in the 20th district! He instantly recognizes me though it is many years since we've seen each other. He gets out and we shake hands, and he says: „Ja, es ist alles gut geworden" ("Yes, everything has turned out well.") (2006).

Those who were lucky to be employed by the municipality were occupied as subway or bus drivers, in garbage removal, in diverse offices, and in gardening. Others have held skilled, low skilled, unskilled jobs, worked in family enterprises, in the service sector, and in the informal sector. Some made money from half-legal or illegal activities. Youths entered, and exited from, apprenticeships, vocational trainings, and a range of funded trainings and courses. Careers have been made – or at least started – in sports, in music, and in dancing. Adolescents also worked in advertising campaigns, fundraising for NGOs, and in insurance and financial investments, where often friends and families are the youth's target groups for their peddling. At present, there are increasingly many jobs with Leihfirmen, personnel leasing firms offering temporary work in a variety of occupations. Older youths drive panel vans, or work in parcel delivery services, the newly established profit-oriented surrogates of former public utilities.

Many of adolescents' jobs are strenuous, low-income, and lack social security, and the youths need to be mobile, flexible, and able to adapt quickly to changing circumstances. In gastronomy and the catering business, a variety of low-paid service jobs are found:

> Su. works as a cocktail mixer in a hotel. He starts work at 4 p.m., going there by bike. He has some days off, but, as he says, irregularly and on short notice only. His previous job had been breakfast preparation in a hotel, where he started at 4 in the morning, cutting fruit and vegetables until 7 or 8 a.m. (2005).

The adolescents' jobs are often on the margins of society and the city. Working hours may be very early, or very late, and far away from the adolescent's living quarters. Many unskilled jobs are in the food industry, and in selling clothes. The adolescents often lose these jobs again:

> Cs. was laid off after having worked at the large supermarket for much of his 17th year. He had been responsible for the sweets and chocolate rack but got transferred to the freezer storage room ("minus 20 degrees"). After becoming ill and having some disputes with his boss, he lost the job. He had just turned 18. Now he is back to "standing in the park" with his peers, as he says. (May 2009).

The decreasing demand for un- and low-skilled work in production – something the park boys, young, strong, eager, would rather like – reduces their options and many adolescents simply stay in the park, drifting in and out of unemployment offices, day labor, and funded training.

In the informal sector, wages are often unpaid. It is also notorious for its health risks, unregulated working hours (very long hours, work on short notice), and heavy labor. There is much irregular work, in mobile phone and internet shops, and in clubs. "The list of precarious jobs is endless and constantly growing" (*Jahresbericht Back on Stage 5*, 2006). The go-go dancers and bouncers in nightclubs are in this class of work.

Park youths tend to lack basic literacy and math skills. Reading is not a favorite pastime with them and even mocked by peers[76]. Basic social skills necessary in urban surroundings for interacting with strangers are often not very well developed. All this, coupled with poverty and the social stigmata against their parents, families, and themselves, do not help them find jobs.

Dual Education System and Apprenticeships

Apprenticeship in the "dual education system", unique to the German speaking countries, is an integral part of the social welfare state, and was developed in the 1960s and 1970s as the "Glanzstück" (masterpiece) of the industrial labor society. It consists of practical learning in a (private) firm or company – apprenticeship – and school education in the Berufsschule (vocational school). The dual education system, alternating one day at Berufsschule with four days at work, is aimed at interweaving schooling with the labor market (Oehme/ Beran/Krisch 2007:59). The apprenticeship is a combined program of real work experience with more inclusive vocational training, and its completion (usually after three years) promises better wages, career options, and prospects, even the possibility of opening up one's own business.

This system is not oriented towards providing a humanistic education (acquiring knowledge and developing the character), but on teaching the vocational-technical skills needed for the labor market. It was closely connected with the industrial labor society, regulated by the social welfare state where full employment was achieved, but "der Strukturwandel der Arbeitsgesellschaft wirkt sich mit voller Wucht auf die Übergänge in Arbeit im Jugend- und jungen Erwachsenenalter aus" ("the structural change of the labor society strongly affects the adolescents' and young adults' transitions into work", Oehme/Beran/ Krisch 2007:63). The park adolescents' experiences show such failed transitional processes.

Ke. had been looking for an apprenticeship for months after finishing school, and had almost given up trying. However, he also gave up his first apprenticeship as a cook: „Ich habe eine Kochlehre angefangen, eineinhalb

---

76 Ana: „Manchmal tu ich auch ein Buch lesen, hihi, oh das ist peinlich." Q.: Das ist peinlich? – Ana: „Ja!" – Q.: Wieso? – Ana: „Mich hat mal eine Freundin ausgelacht, weil ich ein Buch gelesen hab." ("Sometimes I do read a book, hihi, that's embarrassing." – That is embarrassing? – "Yes!" – Why? – "A friend once made fun of me because I read a book.") (Schindlauer 2008:45).

Monate. Die Zeiten haben mich aber gestört, ich bereue es jetzt." ("I started an apprenticeship as a cook, but quit because of the working hours. Now
I regret it.") (Interview 2005).

Adolescents after Hauptschule (junior high school up to 14 years) and Poly-
technikum (an interludial school year until the pupil reaches 15 years, the legal
working age) spend months, often years, searching for an apprenticeship. If it
materializes at all, there was no chance to find out beforehand if it was the right
choice. The youths' wishes connected to such a vocation are usually unrealistic,
uninspired, oriented toward traditional gender roles, and based on rather hazy
ideas of the job market and of society in general.

> De., 17, says that she finished school with good marks three years ago. Af-
> ter a rather difficult time of searching for a job, she finally found an appren-
> ticeship in flower trading, but got laid off last December. She says that since
> then she has been often ill. But she will start her new career as an apprenti-
> ce in "gastro-economy" in a bagel shop, and she looks forward to that! (In-
> terview 2005).

The adolescents do not have much choice over the professions for which these
apprenticeships are the preparation. Most jobs are in the service sector anyway, and the ambitions some youths had to become a car mechanic or a metal
worker usually are not fulfilled as such jobs have more or less vanished, or are
passed on within family networks.

> On the subway, again. I meet Ab., haven't seen her for some time. She is pale
> and looks tired. I ask how she is, what does she do? She has a new job: sales-
> person in a bakery quite far away from where she lives. Why did she leave
> the other job, an apprenticeship? She seemed rather to like it there, a café
> close to her home, nice team? The boss fired her, falsely accusing her of ha-
> ving stolen money from the cashier (2006).

Oehme/Beran/Krisch speak of the "Drehtüreffekt", the revolving door effect:
for each adolescent who enters the work force, another exits into unemployment (2007:80). The erosion of the dual system (apprenticeship with schooling) includes that apprenticeship contracts have become less secure, and results in the hire-and-fire tactics of firms.

Without a positive Hauptschulabschluss (passing marks in junior high school finals), the chances to find one of the much-coveted apprenticeships are low. Many of the park youths are in this position, and they depend on low- or non-skilled work. A temporary but socially stigmatized option is publicly funded training[77].

Funded Training

> Se. has already lost four rather well-paid jobs although he is only 18. He does not want to talk about that and it seems to be very frustrating for him. Presently he is in a course financed by the employment office, where he is being trained as a car mechanic. The cars are just for practice and there are no real customers: for him, it is just a bogus teacher and a bogus job. They don't give him much money, 150 Euro per month, but he acknowledges that they have given him a chance. He often hates getting up in the morning, but „gute und schlechte Zeiten hat jeder Mensch" ("everybody has good and bad times.") He is resigned, and tries to explain his feelings as the general human predicament. "How are you?" – "Right now, I'm good, I'm with my friends." But he says that on other days he would give a different answer: „Es geht mir Scheisse, lass mich in Ruhe." ("I'm fucking bad, leave me alone") (Interview 2005).

Many unemployed adolescents are in such funded trainings, where they may learn a vocation like plumbing, masonry, or carpentry, albeit with a mere pocket money, not the substantially higher apprenticeship wages. But after the course, they have to find a "real" job, which can be very difficult. As a result, motivation in these courses is quite low. And, because of the strict regulations, park kids tend to drop out, which further marginalizes and isolates these "problem kids", cutting them off even more from mainstream society's communication and information – not the way to turn them into solution kids.

Without a vocation or real opportunities, the youth's temporary jobs in service and their hazy ideas about work and the economy result in disappoint-

---

77   „Viel öfter haben diese Maßnahmen für diese Jugendlichen einen stigmatisierenden Effekt, so dass ihre Chancen in der freien Wirtschaft vielfach eher sinken als steigen, und zwar umso mehr, je mehr Maßnahmen sie durchlaufen haben." ("More often, these measures have a stigmatizing effect on these youths, so that their chances in the free economy often decrease, and the more so, the more measures they ran through". Oehme/Beran/Krisch 2007:80).

ment and frustration, and they are easily discouraged. The motivation to stick out difficulties is not high; and specific vocational goals are either not available, or illusory anyway. So they just go along, drifting from one job to the other, like a straw in the river, as Fabrice Plomb (2001) has put it.

Also, the border between legal work and half-legal or illegal jobs is sometimes not clear to the youths in the parks and cages, and their knowledge of employment laws, unions, and social security is insufficient. And unpleasant experiences with the labor market – such as in some wretched job with strangers, who are sometimes mean and sometimes untrustworthy – can make crime and its bosses look attractive to a kid.

Special Circumstances for Some Girls

Some girls vanish from the job market, and after finishing school do not frequent the crowded job centers but stay at home instead, and help around the house and with younger siblings. Their family might even depend on their housework, and do not encourage the girls to look for vocational trainings or jobs. Other girls just give up the search after a short time; they are obviously under less pressure from their families to find a job and given less incentive to do so than the boys: for example Sl., a young man from the Seitstiegen Park group, was promised a driver's license by his father if he found himself an apprenticeship.

Some girls' expectations for the future are not connected to job, work, or career, but rather to those of their partner or future husband. They may want a job for a limited time, but their ambitions in this area are rather conventional: most want to be a hairdresser or beautician, and many take jobs as salespersons[78].

Work in Small Family-Run Enterprises

A new job realm for adolescents opened up in recent years: work in their family's small business enterprises, such as cafés and groceries, butcher shops, bakeries, market stalls, hairdressers, clothing manufactures, cleaning firms, and car repair workshops. Many of these shops are situated in the family's neighborhood.

> Me., 17, refugee boy from Iraq, has spent some months in jail after being busted for several drug-related offences. He and four of his friends were convicted. After his release, he suffered another period of hard drug addiction,

---

78   See also Pichler (2000) on gendered job wishes and profiles, and Digruber on girls in their work situation between hedonism and insecurity (2003:110ff.).

Market stall, Brunnenmarkt, Wien – Ottakring

and came to the park only infrequently to meet his old peers, and to play soccer or basketball. One day he tells us that he now works with his step-father, who runs a small grocery. The shop is quite busy, especially during the mourning month Moharram, and the work is all right for him (2006).

We meet Mo. in the Geheimpark. He is 21 and has his own company, a cleaning firm. I remember that Mo.'s father had thrown a big party for him when he turned 13. He seems to be some big shot, someone special, with a chief-like position in his family (2007).

Sk., 17 years old, has been looking for a job for a long time. His father owns a neighborhood café, which Sk. claims to have managed during the father's absence. He has, according to his own words, supervised the waiters and was in charge of the cash. But he was anyway searching for an apprentice-ship in gastronomy and has held some posts already, but soon left the job or was thrown out due to disrespectful behavior (2004).

Work in their families' shops and enterprises bring a new, profit-oriented outlook to the youth. Neither success in school, nor command of German, is necessary for such work. The parents' self-sufficient attitude – "Look at us: we don't have an education, but we still can make money" – is absorbed by the youth[79].

Of course, many parents who became successful business people motivate their offspring to go into higher education and university. Such adolescents would be seen in the parks only rarely, and they would rather hang out with their peers at home, often over computers and video games, or actively pursuing their studies and career goals. They eventually join the urban crowds and scenes, which increasingly diversify and also include multi-background students' and artists' circles.

Imaginary Homelands and New Destinies

Cs.: Ja, wir haben ihn lange nicht gesehen, er war in der Türkei, seine Eltern wollten das, die haben gesehen, hier das schaut schlecht aus, das wird nix. Er ist nur herumgehängt, hat keine Arbeit gefunden. Die haben dort ein Geschäft … aber es hat nicht geklappt, er ist jetzt wieder da. (Yes, we have not seen him for a long time, he's been in Turkey. His parents wanted him to go. They saw that it did not look good here, this is leading nowhere. He only hung out, did not find a job. They have a shop there … but it did not work out, he is back now.) (Conversation 2009.)

A new development for adolescents from immigrant backgrounds is remigration to the parents' country of origin[80]. It is often the parents', but sometimes the adolescents', wish to "go back home". The new middle classes are making money as entrepreneurs and invest the money in the countries of origin. In some cases, the parents have built a house with shop facilities in the home country, and their children, especially sons, hope for a future in their land of origin. With prospects in Vienna on the wane, illusions of a "Shangri-La" are nourished as the adolescents become oriented towards "imaginary homelands"[81]. This gives them a feeling of superiority towards their park peers, and while still in their Viennese neighborhood, they stand tall and proud, displaying the changed subjectivity of business men-to-be.

The hopes connected to such a successful return "back home" are seldom realized in a way the adolescent imagined beforehand. But they encourage a

---

79   Observations by Senol Akkilic, long-term youth streetworker and team colleague.
80   Background information comes from S. Akkilic.
81   The term is borrowed from Salman Rushdie's essay collection *Imaginary Homelands* (1992), London: Granta Books. 11th printing.

further detachment from Austrian society and loss of interest in the political processes of Vienna, which is not very strong anyway; trust in participatory processes is low. Most interest in politics usually concerns former homelands, but there as well, the youth hold no expectations for possible participation. There is no confidence that they could change anything; and the expression of one's views is not believed to have any significant impact, so possibilities for speaking out are often not taken. This detachment from established political institutions is almost complete. Their feelings of impotence *vis-à-vis* the state and legal institutions, based on ignorance and frustration, are also expressed in how quickly they abandon plans for careers – if they ever even get to the point of formulating plans at all[82].

> One young man of Albanian background, from one of the drug scenes, spoke repeatedly about 'going back' and joining the UCK, the Albanian underground army in the Kosovo. He said that he was only trying to find the money for his travel, and he knew that everything else would be taken care of for him as soon as he reached his destination. Sure enough, he didn't show at Schottenring for some days; and some weeks later one of his friends in the scene already had his photograph – which shows the boy, in military garb, proudly sporting a machine gun (1999).

This example, rare though it may be, nevertheless shows a connection between politicized emotions about a homeland, and the sinister "options" provided by war.

Another option for some youth is further migration, trying to increase their chances by following family members and relatives to yet another country.

> Mh., Ja.'s younger brother from the Seitstiegen group, has returned to Vienna! He had been living with his relatives in Texas for two years, and worked in their mobile phone shop. Everything went all right: in his leisure time he played poker with his cousins and cruised around in cars. With his money he bought a Ford Thunderbird and had it shipped to Europe to sell it here. The expenses of the car have ruined him; he cannot find anybody to sell the car to! He is very unhappy. „Alles ist schief gelaufen" – everything went wrong (2006).

---

82   Such topics of governance are yet to be researched.

Several adolescents follow relatives to new destinations: to the US (Mh. and Ra., who were both born in Karachi), to Canada, to Germany, the Netherlands, Italy, or elsewhere. Some adolescents stay abroad, but others return to Vienna – and to the park, to the old peer group.

Job Troubles

> I phone Sf. He cannot speak now: he is in some car with a new boss and they are going to Burgenland to work. It is a trial job for Sf. Some time later he calls me back: now he is standing on the road in the middle of nowhere! He had started to quarrel with the boss-to-be, who stopped the car and threw him out. He has no idea where he is – I tell him to ask people, but there are none around. I say to ring somebody's door, but there are no houses either. He keeps walking, and finally finds a house with somebody home. They explain the way to the train station so that he can get back to Vienna. Later, in the evening, I meet him, frustrated and angry, with his peers in the Weichmann Park cage.

Sf. was quite bitter after this experience. It was only many months later that he eventually found employment as a helping hand in the warehouse of a food production company, with which he was very happy.

> Km., park boy from Eremit Park, finished the special pedagogic school with difficulties. Being a dedicated soccer player, his days in the cage seemed never-ending, yet he stayed away over time. One day I meet him: "Where are you, moruk[83]?" He found a job in the warehouse of a furniture industry – and even better, his best friend works there too! They manage their daily chores together and although it is hard work, they enjoy their cooperation (2006).

A problem adolescents sometimes have with jobs in mainstream society is the isolation from their peers – something not known in the old factory days when one went to work together with one's friends. The park kids, as young people usually do, long to be together with peers and friends, which is especially important for members of closed groups, such as Sf. and Km. To leave their group, which gives them emotional support, means to go into "enemy territo-

---

83   The Turkish term *moruk* is *Oida* in Viennese; both meaning "old chap".

ry" where bosses and mean colleagues treat them badly. This is a hard break in their lives. If problems at work arise, the way back into the group is easy. It can even be connected with a kind of victorious feeling – especially if the youngster got kicked out after standing up to an older colleague. These experiences make great stories on the park benches. Failures are often retold as success stories, as a youth's resistance against injustice and oppression[84]. It is very hard to judge from the stories whether the cause for the dismissal was the employer's malice or the park youth's fault; but employers' tolerance is low, and many others are waiting for a chance to get the job.

For the adolescents, the focus on work and money begins during school through job counselling and various information offers, and the pupils are still hopeful and self-confident (Oehme/Beran/Krisch 2007:100). After school ends, the job-seeking period can be very long. Feelings of insecurity and dependency increase, and the shortage of jobs results in worry.

> Ja., 18, from the open Seitstiegen group, moved away from the district some time ago and now lives with his younger sisters and his parents in Vienna's outskirts, in a nicer area and better flat. He is polite and friendly, loves Indian food and music, Hindi Movies, and hiphop. Ja. got an apprenticeship as a salesman recently, after a very long period of job-seeking, and a string of courses funded by the employment office. He still comes to the Seitstiegen Park, where he used to spend most of his adolescent years, on his day off or in the evenings, and just like in earlier years, he meets his friends there, they play some basketball and chat, talk to the new, younger park users (Interview 2005).

When people finally succeed in finding a job or apprenticeship after a long and seemingly never-ending period of seeking, this disrupts their park routines. But meeting the park peers is still the main leisure-time activity, and also work further away does not necessarily mean that they discontinue seeing their group's members. But jobs and apprenticeships are not very stable and long-term anyway:

---

84 Both Liebow and Hannerz mention such behavior, not from park benches but from the famous streetcorners: "The streetcorner is … a sanctuary … where failures are rationalized into phantom successes and weaknesses magically transformed into strengths" (Liebow 2003:139). Hannerz speaks of "collective streetcorner mythmaking [which] can at least momentarily ease the burden" (Hannerz 2004:117).

In spite of all good auguries, Ja. lost his apprenticeship as a salesperson. How do I know? Because he suddenly turned up at our office again, after many months. It is always nice to see the kids again – but these circumstances are very sad, yet increasingly frequent: Ke., Yu., Il., Ae., De., now Ja. ... (2007).

Such experiences of fractured careers are increasingly part of all park group members' lives, regardless of their personal skills, school marks, conduct, and family backgrounds. Open groups probably have less inclination to rationalize their failures into successes and therefore might suffer more, take failure more personally than people from closed groups. The predominant feeling adolescents must come to terms with is the feeling that they are neither wanted nor needed. This is real for closed groups since their childhood, and, with recurrent employment failures, increasingly for others as well.

Adolescents in the Music Business

The domain of popular music is profession, money, creativity, and entertainment all rolled into one. Some park adolescents have gained access to the music business, especially young Roma musicians with Balkan and oriental-style music, and some older "gangster and hood" rappers. Others have moved into the music clubs and entertainment places established by people with immigrant backgrounds, and work as DJs. All these developments are part of the new Viennese society, though in still marginalized sectors of it.

Several kids from the park crowds started DJing in youth centers, playing charts R'n'B and hiphop to the other teenagers there. They then moved on to clubs, like the *Jedinstvo* (also for very young teenagers), the large club *Nachtwerk* (with its money rain, parking lot and striptease slanted towards older adolescents and adults), the increasingly numerous Turkish clubs and Bodrum nights, and any number of "oriental-style" discos. There is a rapidly developing scene fostered by, and further encouraging, the cultural and economic diversification of immigrant population groups through entrepreneurship[85].

A singular crossover example of a career in music is the successful Adrian Gaspar Orchestra:

---

85 See also contributions in Gebesmair, Andreas (ed.) (2009), *Randzonen der Kreativwirtschaft. Türkische, chinesische und südasiatische Kulturunternehmungen in Wien.* Wien: LIT Verlag.

Adrian Gaspar, 18, has formed an orchestra from his Musikgymnasium[86] colleagues – who are all well trained and striving for a professional career in classical music – and from friends who are Macedonian Roma based at Katzenpark. The approximately 50 orchestra musicians play a variety of music in a very professional and lively way: Balkan big band sound combined with Bossa Nova, tango, jazz, classical, and rock. The park-based musicians learned their instruments on their own or from relatives. Katzenpark's Er., for example, was trained by his father, a professional clarinet player. Er. played at park parties with his friends since 1999 when they called themselves "Die kleinen Talente" (The Little Talents). – Now Er. plays the clarinet solos in the orchestra, with much approval from the orchestra's classically-trained musicians. (Concert of Adrian Gaspar Orchestra, opening night of the *Balkan Fever Festival*, Szene Wien, April 21st, 2006).

Some adolescents are trained proto-professional musicians (clarinet, drums, keyboards, *saz*), who earn money playing at their community's life-cycle festivities such as henna nights, weddings, and circumcision parties. The profession of musician is often inherited. The children's music training is not usually in music schools or from tutors, but by the parent(s) themselves, who pass their musical traditions on to the children.

Su. came from Sri Lanka with his father as a 12 year-old. His grandfather was a famous musician in Sri Lanka. Su. found friends in the Seitstiegen Park, and they later formed a break dance crew, the Bionic B-Boys. Their approach to life is an open one, their park group sharing both an open view and economic pressure. Su. is a drummer and plays with his father in a reggae band. Reggae is also famous in Sri Lanka in tourist villages like Hikkaduwa. For some time now, the band's success has seemed to grow, and Su. goes on tour with them: they have been to Canada, Paris, Italy, and all over Austria, playing at reggae and Africa festivals and large parties. Not much money comes in, though, and Su. depends on additional jobs. His jobs are temporary also because he needs to leave work if the band has a gig somewhere, and he does neither want to miss the concert, nor to leave the band (2007).

---

86   The Musikgymnasium is a stepping-stone to famous Viennese orchestras.

Many park kids want to become musicians. A career in music becomes even more attractive as chances to find a regular job decline. It probably is easier and more obvious to become a singer or a musician than to attend the Gymnasium. Music can be a meaningful way of sidestepping unsatisfying jobs and economic problems, which seem to be the usual lot in majority society.

d. Park Kids in their Families

The park and cage adolescents' families range from single unemployed parents to rather affluent entrepreneurs. The diversification of the immigrant-background people along lines of politics, financial status, and religion are important influences on the adolescents' attitudes.

Many immigrants obtain Austrian citizenship, which is granted according to length of stay and proven good conduct. As kin groups and communities in Vienna became larger, life-cycle festivities were increasingly celebrated not in the villages "back home", but in Vienna. The migrants' economic position in Vienna also affects the home countries and villages, can alter their families' situation and status through remittances, and class structures in the rural areas, cities and towns are transformed (Mayer 1994).

Post-industrial and global economic changes affect both Austria, as an immigration-receiving country, and the former homelands as the sending countries. Some immigrant families in Vienna face unemployment and a worsening economic situation and this may result in family dissolution and the rupture of contacts with home communities. Others have built up trading firms, mainly in food and clothing, and transnational connections to the former home country for the purposes of import and export are economically important for them and may also improve the back-home families' status.

Political Attitudes and Homeland Politics

The political attitudes of families must be seen in relation to the politics of their (former) homeland, and to the period and the circumstances in which they went away. Many people left Turkey, when the main political problems were the military coups and the suppression of the 1970s liberation and minority movements. Labor migration from what was once Yugoslavia changed to the refugees fleeing war, and the political transformation brought about by post-socialism and nationalism. Divisions among immigrant groups reflect antagonistic political or religious positions, and homeland conflicts. The same is true for refugee families who came from war-torn geopolitical regions such as Chechnya, Iraq, Nigeria, Afghanistan.

Families as social units face many difficulties regarding their members' daily lives. Austrian politics are likely to determine people's lives via such everyday concerns as work permits, unemployment, problems at work, visa regulations, new laws restricting relatives' immigration or visits to Austria, and so on. But (former) homeland politics are more ardently discussed: news are exchanged by telephone, via internet, in cafés, barber shops, and at work. Political positions sometimes result in family quarrels and even family splits, and also define the respective family's relationship to other immigrant groups.

The Adolescents' Approach

Some people of the second or third generation after labor immigration do not want to be seen as torn "between two cultures": it is in fact the "between" which they feel to be their home (see e.g. *Biber, Stadtmagazin für Wien, Viyana und Bec*). Others, such as filmmaker Muzaffer Hasaltay, say:

> The second generation of immigration, of guest workers' children … I am of course reflecting the second generation, because I come from that background as well, I have addressed many topics: family, language, being between societies, being misunderstood, being excluded, or feeling excluded. (M. Hasaltay on his short film *Der Freund*, December 2007).

Or Ra., who came to Vienna from Karachi in 1994, when he was 12 years old. He lives with his parents and younger brother and sisters:

> Ra. feels like a Pakistani, and uses phrases like "in our culture", "for us", "me with a different culture", "I am divided", "I will never be accepted as an Austrian" (Interview 2003).

The Viennese park adolescents of whatever background actively participate in their families' lives. Their political attitudes and opinions, views and values, can be consistent with or different from those prevailing in their families, but will form a new conglomerate. Some groups who feel attracted to neo-national views will be with peers sharing these views (closed groups). Closed groups might keep their sometimes more pointed or radical views from their families, while members of open groups – who probably face a lack of parental understanding when it comes to friendships or lifestyle – try not to infuriate their parents and relatives by expressing their open views at home too often.

I found that even youngsters who emphasize their Muslim beliefs are often ignorant of the religious basics and practice: they are unclear about the differences between Shia and Sunni and the other classical divisions in Islam, and many do not even go to the mosque. Younger teenagers who come in conflict with the law have a heightened awareness of Austrian law and mores. Ethics are frequently discussed among them and with youth workers. Sometimes the Quran's proscriptions, the numerous traditions concerning the Prophet Muhammad's life (typical of Sunni groups), and Wahhabi rules (such as the cutting off thieves' hands) are contrasted with the Austrian legal system.

Some adolescents came as refugees, either with their families, or as unaccompanied minors. They sometimes have an increased interest in the geo-politics connected with and influencing their former home regions. Information on homelands and world politics is sought from media, and mainly from the internet, and shared among groups in coffee shops, private gatherings, and on park benches.

Refugees often have a long journey behind them, and memories of their homelands might be sparse and blurred. Some spent their childhood and early adolescent years on the way. They cannot go home and refresh their impressions. But for the offspring of the labor migrants, frequent and regular trips "home" are not unusual.

Young Migrants' Experiences in their Places of Origin

In the office with Ka. We talk about his summer in Macedonia, from where he has just returned. There is usually one certain day in July when all of a sudden the groups from Katzenpark are gone: they travel to Pr. to spend the summer. They go to the disco Medusa, just as in Vienna they attend the Jedinstvo and the Nachtwerk. However, Ka. is back, and upon my asking about his relatives – how do they live, is there enough food, do they have land to farm on? – Ka. starts slowly, reluctantly, and finally, with a sneer, half-ashamed, he says: "I don't know, the people there … they're not like we are, they do not have … they do not have any culture" (Conversation in 2005).

This is a remark frequently heard from adolescents who have spent the summer in a town or village in their parent's homeland. It seems that the youths see their relatives as "backward", e.g. regarding the former Yugoslavian countries, where the ongoing economic problems leave many living in poverty and deprivation.

Trips to the home countries depend on the family's economic situation, upon the political circumstances in the country, and upon the family's attitude towards their homeland. Rarely is the whole family able to go, and various difficulties are entailed in these larger family gatherings either in villages, small towns, or cities: complaints about the village, political and religious disputes, discussions on chores and who should perform them, unwillingness to comply with rural household life, and more (Mayer 1994).

Sometimes one parent takes the younger children on a trip to the homeland, which is difficult because children do not easily adapt to the change in food and water. Also debates on how to raise children are frequent between home-country elders and migrant parents.

Occasionally, adolescents go on their own, which may be demanding for all those involved. Often after some time their relatives' initially friendly and expectant attitudes toward them change, and they shun the new arrivals, which do not fit into the village or the neighborhood, and the relatives in the homeland discourage a re-visit. Or, the adolescents have no interest in the home families, who they find boring or backward, and who in turn tend to criticize them. Different rules of conduct and of personal mobility and visibility are not easy for the Viennese adolescents to adapt to. They're often unfit to help with complicated, or boring and repetitive, agricultural and domestic chores, they talk back, get into trouble with the local youths, and more.

One common experience the adolescents have when visiting back home is the language barrier, because their command of the mother tongue is rusty and limited. They often have an accent to which their homeland family might react negatively, or they cannot speak the local dialect, and are not well understood in their hometowns. Sometimes they are mocked due to their "affected" language.

Some adolescents, especially if they failed on the labor market in Vienna, have remigrated. In some cases, parents built houses back home and try to establish a transnational business, where they plan to involve the family's older adolescents. The inexperienced youths, unacquainted with local people, customs, and with such work and work in general, fail. The promised, hoped-for subjectivity of a successful businessman or -woman is shattered: back to the parks in Vienna.

Some families are also increasingly interested to visit tourist sites instead of staying with relatives, especially in Turkey:

> Ke. came to Vienna at age 2 or 3. His last visit to Turkey, sightseeing, had
> been the year before, and it was beautiful. But he says, „Ich hab mich wie ein
> Fremder gefühlt" ("I felt like a stranger"). He feels that his home is Vienna
> rather than Turkey, although he does not like his life in Austria very much
> (Interview 2003).

Sometimes, especially when visiting tourist sites, like Ke., the holidaying adolescents feel "like a stranger, like a tourist". They experience a status new to
them, as rich foreign Westerners and European guests *vis-à-vis* the indigenous
people who work in the big hotels and the tourist industry business, and who
sometimes show their contempt for them. This position is antithetical to that
which they have in Vienna, where they are regarded as poor and economically
stressed aliens from an impoverished country, and are underprivileged and often discriminated against.

> When Sf. was in Sivas (Turkey), he got ill, he says, because of the "different
> water and air" ("anderes Wasser und Luft"), and he does not want to visit
> there again. Sf. adheres to neo-national ideas and wears the emblem of the
> Grey Wolves; his unpleasant experiences in Turkey did not alter his politi-
> cal views (Interview 2005).

Adolescents who do go "back" for holidays often find themselves confronted
with negative experiences which do not fit into their preconceived notions of
what their country of origin is like. For example, their parents often are enthusiastic about "the fresh water and air in the village": but these recollections can
sometimes be nostalgic glorifications.

Adolescents' experiences in their homelands are often frustrating, and not easy
to digest. While this must also be seen in the context of their coming of age,
when everything is open to question and looked at from new perspectives, rapid social and economic changes might also account for their difficulties. On
the other hand, the former homelands can become closer because of the transnational business activities of their families, lower travel fares, and the increased use of virtual communication with family members back home. And with
frequent stays in the former home country – for example in a city rather than in
the village –, it is not unlikely that one or the other adolescent might eventually
succeed in establishing a new life there.

e. Park Kids at School

School is obligatory in Austria for kids up to 15 years of age. Whether a school is good or bad in terms of the education it provides depends to a large part on the headmaster and the teachers who, in obligatory schools free of charge, have to bear all the city's "scourges" (to use Southall's term).

> Cs.: „Ja, und dann hab ich die Schule gewechselt für die vierte Klasse, und dort war ein Lehrer, der hat mir geholfen. Nur wegen ihm hab ich gelernt, noch ein halbes Jahr. Dann hab ich den Hauptschulabschluss gehabt." ("Yes, and then I changed school, to attend the 4th grade, and there was a teacher, he helped me. I studied only because of him, for half a year. And so I completed my junior high finals.") (Conversation in 2009).

This is not an exceptional story: many kids who managed to finish school successfully gave the credit to one particular teacher who took a liking to them, supported them, and, if necessary, gave them another chance and stood up for them. Thus success in school frequently may depend upon one teacher and his or her special dedication to a particular student, often during the teacher's free time. Sh., an 11 year-old girl from a refugee background, said:

> Meine Lehrerin hilft mir immer. Sie hat mir gezeigt, wie man zeichnet, und mir Farben geschenkt. Und sie singt auch mit mir. Sie hat mir Unterricht gegeben. Ich will Menschenrechtsanwältin werden. (My teacher always helps me. She showed me how to draw, and gave me crayons. And she sings with me. She taught me and gave me lessons. I want to become a human rights attorney.) (Conversation, summer 2007).

And although such support is important and admirable, successful schooling should not depend upon whether or not a student is liked and supported by a particular teacher.

As has been mentioned, girls interested in pursuing higher education tend to avoid the parks, where they feel their intellectual aspirations are not supported. Also their parents might oppose further education for them. The girls often find themselves in arguments with their parents and former peers, trying to defend their educational goals.

After years without hearing from her, we meet Mü. again. She tells us, happily, that she just passed her Matura (senior high school exams)! We are extremely impressed; she had to fight hard and continually for this against her family, who did not want her to attend school that long. Now she hopes to study to become a medical doctor. But first, in the summer, she must work. Her mother lives in the Netherlands and is divorced from Mü.'s father who, with his new wife, treats her and her brother badly. The brother, Km., is a cage-group boy proper who finished special elementary school only after some difficulties. (Summer 2007).

The number of park-based adolescents in higher education has been very small. Most go to Hauptschule (junior high school), or to special supporting pedagogic centers (where up to 100 percent have non-German speaking parents), and many stop going to school altogether at an early age. And leaving school at 15 does not necessarily mean the student completed school: some leave after the 2nd grade of Hauptschule, having attended both grades twice and therefore are already 14 or 15 years old. Many of the student's subjects might not be evaluated at all ("nicht beurteilt", mostly due to poor attendance), or judged as "not satisfactory" ("nicht genügend") in their final school reports.

The deferred gratification pattern necessary for embarking in higher education is often not possible in poorer population groups. Families depend on their adolescents' contribution to family income and want their children to enter the labor market as soon as possible. Moreover, low-skilled or unskilled parents and relatives are not acquainted with higher, let alone university education, and they cannot or will not support their children with the privacy and space necessary for homework, nor with the money required to continue schooling. Language skills, writing, reading, and mathematics are least likely to be mastered by children and youth from such backgrounds, including majority children whose performance at school often is not better, and sometimes a lot worse, than that of their immigrant classmates.

Parks can be recreational places for meeting after school. But parks can also be places where, because of truancy or temporary expulsion, the adolescent goes instead of school. Because school, as Albert Cohen has stated, evokes feelings of exclusion and the fear of failure to meet standards, the alternative of the free park life and the group autonomy of the park groups looks much more attractive to park kids, whose interaction with social mainstream realms further decreases.

For those still enrolled at school but hanging out somewhere else, there is also the necessity to avoid the notice and attention of teachers, parents, and police, and they escape from the district and the parks during the day. The large funfair areas and open grounds of the Wiener Prater and the Böhmische Prater are good places to pass the time, and for making new contacts with other groups, winning or losing money at games, for meeting girls, or for getting into fights. "Bad boys" expelled from school head into uncontrolled common urban spaces and expand their knowledge of "bad boy" pastimes.

Stephansplatz from above; breakers in front

Results and Conclusions

Parks as Arena

Adolescents feel that parks and cages are places where they can live their own lives, and engage in sports activities, meetings, discussions, and other group-based pastimes. As a marked difference to childhood, these activities are increasingly self-determined and less restricted by adults and institutions. Adolescents thus claim "their parks" and their right to live as they like. Parks are almost free of adult control, and the relevant groups establish the park rules by themselves (if not always democratically). Escape and evasion (from police, parents, youth institutions etc.) is easy in the parks, and parks are good places for a wide variety of experiences, which can be termed fragmented and self-initiations. Parks can also become a youth's first contact zone with violence, incipient youth gang formation and illegal activities, and forms of prostitution.

Park life goes on: while older "parkers" are still around, at least in their minds, children have grown up and followed in their footsteps. New groups come to Vienna claiming space, adding their own histories to the oral chronicles of the parks and cages. The tales of people and their experiences of living on society's margins are a collective memory shared by park kids. Throughout one district, and often far beyond, park youth know each other.

Parks are used by adolescents for their interests, while co-existing with other users and groups in conflict, compromise, and consensus. As part of public, communal space, parks are devalued compared to private and privileged space. The parks influence park youths' position in their other spatial and social contexts and in wider society. Parks are therefore also symbolic of exclusion.

The excluded park spheres are arenas where the actual struggles in society take place, symbolically, and also where "the chips are down" (Turner 1994:134) for struggles and fights among and between the groups but also with, and within, society at-large. It is from the margins that societies can open up, because it is there that power relations, structures of exclusion, and unjust conditions become visible. The very existence of parks as marginalized public space, and of park kids as marginalized urban groups, points to exclusion mechanisms in the political field.

Parks are both a retreat for groups and a public stage. The parks are an integral part of society, neither set apart from nor independent of Vienna. Parks, and parks as arenas, are most of all the sites of park youths' struggle for recognition as part of the whole.

Results of Research Questions

Groups

Groups, formed in the neighborhood or through kinship during childhood, often persist far into adulthood. For many, they remain the most important social relation. All adolescents in parks are with one or the other group. The peer groups, the friendships, and the often long-lasting relationships in larger groups of like-minded people are *Gemeinschaft* in *Gesellschaft*.

Kids in the park are boys and girls who make use of the parks to meet and to play. Many of them are boys for whom soccer is important. Girls often leave the neighborhood parks with their coming of age, being denied park space by boys and by conventional restrictions; or they leave if they enter higher education. Some older girls enter a park's life either as a leisure time activity, following new friends, or when looking for a retreat from home. The considerable differences among parks concerning the girls' presence usually are connected with the groups frequenting a particular park. Park boys sometimes think of their own parks as "bad" and do not want their sisters, girlfriends, or cousins to be there.

I classify park "residents" – that is, those who use one park regularly – into "open" and "closed" groups. Open groups expand their radius of action into common urban space, where they meet new people and have new experiences. Closed groups share an in-group worldview, and tend towards neo-nationalist outlooks and sometimes, violent behavior. The models of "open" and "closed" groups are not mutually exclusive categories; they are instead models of attitude trends which shift and change, sometimes remarkably fast. Fusion and fission processes are often due to such attitudes and evolving differences in worldviews. The type of a group a youth belongs to determines his or her further mobility in the neighborhoods and the common urban spaces. In their open groups, the adolescents enter the larger urban crowds and scenes, and the consumer world. Closed groups are often excluded from these realms, to which they react violently. The provision of economic resources for a group's members marks incipient gangs.

The peer group is an emotional and intellectual resource and retreat, but can also become an obstacle for social mobility. However, both open and closed groups' options for economic and political participation are meagre. As A. Southall maintained, "gangs decrease with employment"; the corollary of this is that gangs *in*crease with unemployment. Although I met only a few incipient gangs, there is good reason to think that, as job options and general prospects of youth decline, gangs proper will form.

Interaction with Vienna's Majority Society

Schools are communication bridges where information on society at-large is offered, and, apart from basic education and access to knowledge, also afford pupils the opportunity to take part in school projects, democracy workshops, excursions, and day trips out into the community. Conversely, society at-large is influenced through schools, as the pupils' life circumstances and experiences, their problems and opinions, and their newly forming outlooks and positions are communicated via teachers and their interactions with other sectors of society. Attending school is a way of speaking in society. But barriers to education are many and high; park kids drop out easily, only a few youths make it into higher education, and those who do, will eventually leave the park groups behind.

The school careers of many park kids are not unbroken by truancy, expulsion, lack of interest and frustration. But even if they do well, the school-to-work transition is often ruptured by the increasingly difficult integration into the "flexible" labor market. Alternatives to the official labor market become more important to park youths: these include funded trainings, jobs and probably careers in sports and in the music and entertainment businesses, in family enterprises, the informal sector, as well as illegal activities.

Work is often connected with bitter experiences for park adolescents. Sucked in through the "revolving door" into work or its under-paid surrogates (funded training), they often find themselves confronted with unfriendly bosses and co-workers. When they are fired – which frequently occurs – they easily fall back into their groups, and fictionalize "failure into success", as the ghetto groups on Liebow's and Hannerz' streetcorners did. These – and other – similarities between ghetto streetcorners and Viennese park benches might point to an increasing economic and social exclusion of park kids, and to emergent racialization among juveniles in central Europe.

Park youths on the job front are dealing mainly, if not exclusively, with working-class people, often also from immigrant backgrounds. Few park kids of any background have contact with Viennese middle- and upper class groups. Park adolescents are likely to be ignorant of Viennese majority social structures, and of cultural institutions. Nobody among the Viennese park kids would go to the Opera; and most don't even know where it is[87]. The parents of some park youth are from middle-class background in their homelands – but they have rarely managed to maintain that status in Vienna.

Some park kids have early encounters with the law through juvenile delinquency. Thanks to the welfare system in Austria, these adolescents can be sure of getting at least some money and support through education and job training programs. Gang formation is thus still largely held at bay.

Park adolescents' drug uses reflect their reluctant attitude towards the Austrian mainstream. They almost ignore alcohol, whether because they are Muslim, or out of a more general disapproval, shared by (majority) hiphoppers, and majority cannabis smokers. Through the latter, park kids come into

---

87 Both Hannerz and Liebow remarked identically about the Washington D.C. downtown ghetto neighborhoods, that they were "within walking distance of the White House" (Liebow 2003:10; Hannerz 2004:211). Liebow goes on: "... if anyone cared to walk there, but no one ever does."

contact with majority people who obviously hold alternative views on society and their own position in it, being criminalized as users.

Integration means that all groups in society are part of the whole. The park youths' economic, cultural, social, and political contributions must be recognized. These include their critique – however inexpert, multi-vocal, or speechless – of injustice and (institutionalized) marginalization.

The Background of Immigration

Adolescents in parks come from numerous backgrounds, and many have an immigration history, which results in a basic solidarity, a basic sharing and understanding of each other's experiences in growing up: racism, "blaming the victims", barriers to education, and being misunderstood.

Adolescents view Vienna and their or their parents' former homelands in a variety of ways[88]:

- A few youths feel Vienna to be their home, where they wish to participate in urban life (such adolescents frequent the parks only temporarily).

- Others find Vienna to be their home because there is, unfortunately, no other. But they lack prospects, opportunities and approval in Vienna, so they must come to terms with being here.

- Others find themselves between two cultures. They try out both options, but often find that neither works; the "between" has become home.

- A fourth group tries to remodel their Viennese neighborhood – a relatively safe place for them – into "back home" by staying in homeland-type surroundings (coffeehouse, work in the family shop, closed park group).

- And a fifth group wants to transform "back home" – to which they might eventually re-migrate or aspire to do so – into Vienna, or what they know of Vienna. They are bound to run into trouble as people back home reject them and their attitudes, which are regarded as alien, arrogant, and provoking.

Park adolescents' backgrounds do not dominate their feelings, attitudes, values; most are from poor homes, live in small flats without much homeland

---

88 Many adolescents, of course, will go through changing views, and shift between these variations.

culture about, apart from the odd family picture. Generally, their families blend into a global working-class. Adolescents' experiences in their relatives' homelands are also limited, and they usually are not aware of, or do not gain access to, the newly forming cosmopolitan cohorts of young middle classes and nouveau-riches in the rapidly changing countries of the families' origin.

Generally *all* young people in Vienna are coming of age in circumstances inseparably linked to the history of labor migration and refugee movements to Vienna. Park youth scenes are part of society's struggle to open up. Like the Caribbean immigrants to Great Britain, "Gastarbajteri"[89] have come to the front to speak out and to insist on having their participation in society recognized, and their contributions to Austria's development acknowledged.

Urban Youth – Youth in Cities

Youth in cities are vulnerable groups and they depend, for their development towards maturity, on favorable surroundings. These include the opportunity for open interactions and communication with as many different people as possible. To form and strengthen connections with the wider society, they must be able to see, meet, and observe other people, and have the prospects of organizing their own new world. Their social, economic, political, and cultural achievements and their enjoyment of the emotions and activities of their coming of age must be seen as part of the whole, welcome and accepted.

Cities as concentrated spheres of human potentialities may offer all these opportunities. But counteracting forces are at work: the separation and segregation of young people into special locations; denial of access to economic production and consumption; under- and over-demand in school, education, and jobs; and rejection from the dominant social order due to essentialized ethnic and working-class backgrounds.

The subject-based mind-body developments can neither be separated from the urban conditions, nor from their new position in society. Being young, poor and rejected in the oecumenopolis shape the young people's experiences during childhood, puberty, and growing up.

There are two main ways of dealing with these conditions, of acting in these conditions: an open way – urban, post-racial and post-migrant, striving for intergroup solidarity, and togetherness. And a closed way, adhering to the still dominant global practices of racism, inner-group solidarity, and gang mentality.

---

89   Exhibition title and publication (Gürses and Kogoj, eds., 2004).

HipHop Grows! Work in Progress. Einsiedlerpark 1997

Global Urban Society

Adolescents in cities who belong to the working-class population in the global urban society are increasingly left without substantial participation in production processes. Feelings of exclusion and marginalization are part of park adolescents' urban experiences in growing up. Bodily practices and styles express and reflect these experiences. All such manifestations are intertwined with global society both ways: by taking up the mass-mediated offers, styles, and ideas; and by sending pictures back through virtual channels, successful culture production, and by being seen and scene. Dwelling in virtual realities is a further connection to globality through information on war, music, and through computer games and their designs.

Park adolescents are connected to global processes through transnationality, global popular music, television and internet uses, consumer lifestyles, and body images. The international contexts forged by migration movements are newly experienced and formed by adolescents' visits to their parents' home countries, and some follow their families' and relatives' transnational flows further abroad. The transnational stretch that many of Vienna's park-based adolescents live reacts with global economic integration.

World politics enter their spheres, often with post-racial, post-national and post-migrant approaches, but also with neo-nationalism, i.e. neo-national ideologies under "different global and transnational conditions" (Gingrich and Banks 2006:2), and sometimes neo-religious views: the new forms of religiosity under present-day geopolitical realities, that also include the impacts of 9/11.

Through music, park kids have absorbed an image of "ghetto", of the Bronx and Los Angeles, and many share Michael Jackson's complaint that "they don't really care about us". Looking at park youths' most precious musical interests, an implicit resistance to the surrounding majority society is entailed in them: arabesk, Balkan musical traditions, the open aggressiveness of gangsta rap, the globally mixed R'n'B, R'n'Besk, and Bhangra express youths' insisting on plurivocality. Black music, especially rap, is a model for expressing and representing experiences and, as in particular the black stars did and do, for demanding to be heard and recognized as partaking in and shaping the forces of history.

Viennese parks can hardly be seen as ghettos. But parks can turn into an imagined ghetto for youths: spatial representations of a globally mediated concept, containing experiences of precarity, oppression, exclusion, and poverty, and also poor-on-poor crime and immobility both in social and spatial terms.

Park Youth's Ethnography in the Light of Academic Literature

The literature I use centers on youth in urban conditions of poverty, apart from the works of M. Mead (first published in 1928) and Schlegel/Barry (1991), which are windows into societies before global urbanism.

Watson and the authors in his anthology (1977) have researched immigrant groups on both ends of the migration chain. Park youth feel more solidarity with those in the same minority position of exclusion than with former home-society's localities. This is consistent with observations by the contributors to Watson's volume, especially by the Ballards and by Nancy Foner.

Lack of jobs and no access to legally earned money will probably encourage gang formation, the process of which is discussed in Thrasher's (first published in 1927) and Cohen's (1955) books. Formed during early childhood on a neighborhood base, many of the park groups persist until adulthood. Although Vienna park groups rarely become gangs, the gang mentality observed by Thrasher is found in some groups.

Cohen explains adolescents' preference for autonomous group life as a reaction to the frustrations brought about by society's norms and demands the boys cannot meet. In Vienna's parks, such frustrations are strongly felt. Members of open groups are likely to find the reasons for their and others' exclusion in racism and nationalism and also in an individual's attitudes; closed groups tend to explanations based on essentialized notions of society, ethnicity and religion.

Both Thrasher and Cohen mention parents' inability to understand their children's social needs. This is true for park adolescents as well, but the diversity of families with immigrant backgrounds entails a multitude of attitudes, coherent with a family's political and economic standing. Accordingly, different approaches, explanations, and also solutions and support for their children will be offered.

Looking at London under the circumstances of post-colonialism, a recessional economy, and declining welfare, Gilroy (first published in 1987) took us on a tour through sub-cultural activism of global impact: punk rock and reggae against racism. Music does have an important position for adolescents in Vienna; music production, often with their families, has been shown to hold job opportunities for them. While musical styles are preferred which contain positions opposed to Austria's mainstream and are critical of majority society, definite political activism as mentioned by Gilroy is not often found among park youth.

Helena Wulff (1995) observed girls in South London to be in the forefront of ethnic mixture and post-racial thinking. In Vienna, girls in pairs and groups are spatially and socially mobile at a younger age, meet more people, and are less dominated by group structures than park boys who are closely affiliated with a certain park or cage group. (*Why* girls must stray further, being denied the necessary spaces for play and interaction in their surroundings, is less positive.) But generally, not just the girls, but most members of open groups express their attitudes through dress, style, and symbols – bodily manifestations of a post-ethnic view.

Baumann's study (1996) shows how the "dominant discourse" of culture and community, which introduces categories of segregation and discrimination, takes hold of population groups, and determines their perceptions of themselves and others as "ethnic". Baumann finds that adolescents came to more fluid categories through new ways of integrating their experiences. Viennese park adolescents are subjected to, and stigmatized and essentialized by, the dominant discourse. Open or closed groups deal differently with these mediated exclusion mechanisms: open groups by mobility among an urban crowd; closed groups through retreat, violence, and seclusion.

Sassen (1995), Gingrich and Banks (2006), and Ivekovic (2008) point to hidden structures, which still guide present-day European societies. Countries cling to their imperial and colonial past and (neo-colonial) present. Rotenberg (1995) maintains that the urban landscape mirrors people's views of social relationships. The parks, then, appear as realms of an "alien", stand-by work force.

Concluding Remarks

I have looked at varied immigration patterns. People moved to cities and metropolitan areas from colonial realms, from former colonies, and from the internal and external countryside: to Chicago from the rural South and from Catholic Europe; to Great Britain from Jamaica; and to France from North Africa. But these distinct patterns lead to similar conditions for urban youths: exclusion, barriers to education, denied access to more rewarding economic spheres; the youths' contact only with controlling figures, and their nebulous view of the surrounding majority society. There are, in any city and metropolitan area, those most deprived youths who act and re-act with and against their stigmata; some get tangled in self-fulfilling prophecies and might be in groups appearing "mad, bad, and dangerous to know" ... as Phillips and Phillips remark on the white, working-class Teddy Boys in England's 1950s (1999:161).

Accordingly, youth group formations are also similar: sticking together, doing things together, hanging out together, making music, and expressing their experiences. Park adolescents who insist on being together in their groups try to live this *communitas* both as a "bond uniting ... people over and above any formal or social bonds" (Turner 1994:45), and in dialogue, conflict, or struggle with "structure" or *societas*. The park kids are: "betwixt and between" spatially, socially, symbolically: through the transitory phase of youth; between national and economic cultures; between the need to consume and the inability to do so, but also on the forefront of those "die leben und kämpfen für den Eros gegen den Tod" ("who live and fight for Eros and against death", Marcuse in Brunkhorst/Koch:93).

The anthropological study of youth in cities shows how neither of these groups can be explained by their "cultural" or "ethnic" backgrounds. It is rather the urban surroundings that lead to these formations under conditions of insecurity and poverty; those from undocumented and labor migration streams are usually involved in the most deprived groupings. It is urban anthropology, which has shown that cities – developed from a new economic productivity (Ansari and Nas 1983) – have been, from their very beginning, "the central arena on which the fateful drama of human wealth and inequality has been played" (Southall 2000:14). My present study is one more contribution to this drama.

All adolescent park groups come into existence as an urban phenomenon in global conditions. Society's development comes from its margins, from those demanding recognition, rights, and participation. The population groups who expose the hidden asymmetries, who point to injustice and exclusion, also show new prospects.

Las Vegas. Graffiti detail, Einsiedlerpark

Bibliography

Amin, Ash and Thrift, Nigel (2002), *Cities. Reimagining the Urban*. Oxford: Blackwell.

Amit-Talai, Vered and Wulff, Helena (eds.) (1995), *Youth Cultures. A Cross-Cultural Perspective*. London: Routledge.

Ansari, Ghaus and Nas, Peter (1983), Introduction. In Ansari and Nas (eds.), *Town-Talk. The Dynamics of Urban Anthropology*. Leiden: Brill, pp. 1–6.

Arslan, Savas (2011), *Cinema in Turkey. A New Critical History*. New York et al.: Oxford University Press.

Ballard, Roger and Ballard, Catherine (1979), The Sikhs: The Development of South Asian Settlements in Britain. In Watson (ed.), pp. 21–56.

Baumann, Gerd (1996), *Contesting Culture. Discourses of identity in multi-ethnic London*. Cambridge: Cambridge University Press.

Becker, Howard S. (1963), *Outsiders. Studies of a Sociology of Deviance*. New York: The Free Press.

Behera, Deepak and Trawick, Margaret (eds.) (2007), *Children and Youth in the Global Metropole*. New Delhi: Manak.

Benard, Cheryl and Schlaffer, Edit (1999), Die weggespielten Mädchen. In Verein Jugendzentren der Stadt Wien (ed.), pp. 49–56.

Bestor, Theodore C. (2004), *Tsukiji. The Fishmarket at the Center of the World*. Berkeley et al.: University of California Press.

Biber. Stadtmagazin für Wien, Viyana und Bec (February 2008), Echte Wiener: Gangsta Rap ist in Wien gelandet – Sua Kaan, Stonepark 12 und Becka Sekta. Ivana Cucujkić, Bernhard Gaul and Daniel Shaked (photos), pp 34–40. www.dasbiber.at. Biber Verlagsgesellschaft mbH, 1070 Wien (ed.).

Binder, Susanne (2004), *Interkulturelles Lernen aus ethnologischer Perspektive. Konzepte, Ansichten und Praxisbeispiele aus Österreich und den Niederlanden*. Wien: LIT Verlag.

Binder, Susanne, Seiser, Gertraud, Streissler, Anna (2004), Anthropology of Education and Organisational Systems. In Khittel, Plankensteiner, Six-Hohenbalken (eds.), pp. 126–149.

Blum, Johanna and Kromer, Ingrid (2009), Deprived Young People Struggling for Resources and Recognition in a Densely Built Quarter: Urbanitz, Austria. In Riepl and Williamson (eds.), pp. 131–166.

Böhnisch, Lothar and Schröer, Wolfgang (2007), Der Auftrag der Jugendarbeit im Strukturwandel der Arbeitsgesellschaft – ein Nachwort. In Oehme, Beran, Krisch, pp. 173–181.

Bourdieu, Pierre (1997), *Méditations pascaliennes*. Paris: Seuil.

—   (2000 [1977]), *Die zwei Gesichter der Arbeit. Interdependenzen von Zeit- und Wirtschaftsstrukturen am Beispiel einer Ethnologie der algerischen Übergangsgesellschaft*. Konstanz: UVK.

—   (ed.) (2001), *Der Lohn der Angst. Flexibilisierung und Kriminalisierung in der "neuen Arbeitsgesellschaft"*. Int. Jahrbuch für Literatur und Kultur 99/00, Konstanz: UVK.

Brunkhorst, Hauke and Koch, Gertrud (no year indicated), *Herbert Marcuse. Eine Einführung*. Wiesbaden: Junius Verlag.

Brown, Peter L. (ed.) (1998), *Understanding and Applying Medical Anthropology*. Mountain View: Mayfield Publ.

Budka, Philipp and Kremser, Manfred (2004), CyberAnthropology – Anthropology of CyberCulture. In Khittel, Plankensteiner and Six-Hohenbalken, pp. 213–226.

Cahnman, Werner J. (1981), Tönnies in Amerika. In Lepenies (ed.), pp. 82–114.

Carr, Rocky (1998), *brixton bwoy. A novel*. London: Fourth estate.

Cohen, Albert K. (1967 [1955]), *Delinquent Boys: The Culture of the Gang*. 12th printing. New York: The Free Press.

Dany, Hans-Christian (2009), *Speed. Eine Gesellschaft auf Droge*. Edition Nautilus. Hamburg: Lutz Schulenburg.

Davis-Sulikowski, Ulrike and Khittel, Stefan (2004), Socio-Cultural Anthropology after the Imperial Turn: Diaspora and Postcolonial Studies. In Khittel, Plankensteiner and Six-Hohenbalken (eds.), pp. 83–107.

Diederichsen, Diedrich (1995), Wie aus Bewegungen Kulturen und aus Kulturen Communities werden. In Fuchs, Moltmann and Prigge (eds.), pp. 126–139.

Dilek, Cinar, Gürses, Hakan, Herzog-Punzenberger, Barbara, Reiser, Karl, and Strasser, Sabine (1999), *Konfrontationen: Identitätsprozesse Jugendlicher von unterschiedlicher Herkunft in Wien*. Wien: Endbericht des Projektteams.

Digruber, Daniela (2003), *Mädchen der 2. Generation im dualen Ausbildungssystem. Berufsfindungsprozesse, Zufriedenheit und Zukunftsaussichten*. Diploma work, Universität Wien.

Eames, Edwin and Goode, Judith Granich (1977), *Anthropology of the City. An Introduction To Urban Anthropology*. Englewood Cliffs: Prentice-Hall.

Eisenbach-Stangl, Irmgard, Bernardis, Alexander, Fellöcker, Kurt, Haberhauer-Stidl, Judith and Schmied, Gabriele (2008), *Jugendliche Alkoholszenen. Konsumkontexte, Trinkmotive, Prävention*. Europäisches Zentrum für Wohlfahrtspolitik und Sozialforschung. Wien.

Encyclopedia of Cultural Anthropology (1996), Levinson, David and Ember, Melvin (eds.), New York: Henry Holt & Co.

Encyclopedia of Social and Cultural Anthropology (1996), Barnard, Alan and Spencer, Jonathan (eds.), London and New York: Routledge.

Encyclopedia of Social Theory (2006), Harrington, Austin, Marshall, Barbara, Müller, Hans-Peter (eds.), London and New York: Routledge.

Expedition Jugend-Zone. Sozialraumanalyse Ottakring 2010. Verein Wiener Jugendzentren.

Feest, Christian and Kohl, Karl-Heinz (eds.) (2001), *Hauptwerke der Ethnologie*. Stuttgart: Alfred Kröner Verlag.

Förster, Kirsten, Gruber, Sonja, Hingsamer, Rosi, Mayrhofer, Rita, Mayer, Danila (2002), Platz da! Mädchen im öffentlichen Raum. In Verein FluMiNut (ed.), Wissen_schaf(f)t Widerstand: Dokumentation des 27. Kongresses von Frauen in Naturwissenschaft und Technik. Wien: Milena Verlag, pp. 250–255.

Foner, Nancy (1979), The Jamaicans: Cultural and Social Change among Migrants in Britain. In Watson (ed.), pp. 120 – 150.

Freeman, Derek (1999), *The Fateful Hoaxing of Margaret Mead. A Historical Analysis of her Samoan Research.* Boulder: Westview Press.

Fuchs, Gotthard, Moltmann, Bernhard, and Prigge, Walter (eds.) (1995): *Mythos Metropole.* Frankfurt am Main: Suhrkamp.

Gächter, Martin (2000), *Rap und Hip-Hop. Geschichte und Entwicklung eines afrikanisch-amerikanischen "Widerstandsmediums", unter besonderer Berücksichtigung seiner Rezeptionsformen in Österreich.* Diploma work, Universität Wien.

The Gale Encyclopedia of Childhood and Adolescence (1998), Kagan, Jerome and Gall, Susan B. (eds.), Detroit et al.: Gale.

Geisler, Marion (1996), *Mädchenfreundschaften. Die Bedeutung der besten Freundin in der weiblichen Adoleszenz, eine empirische Studie.* Diploma work, Universität Wien.

Gelder, Ken (ed.) (2005), *The Subcultures Reader.* 2nd edition. London: Routledge.

Giedion, Siegfried (1987 [Mechanization Takes Command, 1948]), *Die Herrschaft der Mechanisierung. Ein Beitrag zur anonymen Geschichte.* Gebundene Sonderausgabe. Bodenheim: Athenaeum.

Gilroy, Paul (2000 [1987]), *'There Ain't No Black in the Union Jack'. The cultural politics of race and nation.* London: Routledge.

Gingrich, Andre and Banks, Marcus (eds.) (2006), *Neo-nationalism in Europe and Beyond. Perspectives from Social Anthropology.* New York: Berghahn Books.

Großegger, Beate, Heinzlmaier, Bernhard, and Zentner, Manfred (eds.) (1999), *Trendpaket 3. Jugendkultur 2000.* Österreichisches Institut für Jugendforschung. Graz – Wien: Zeitpunkt.

Gruber, Sonja (1999), *Nutzungsanalyse des Einsiedlerparks und des Sankt-Johann-Parks.* Wien: Im Auftrag der Leitstelle für alltags- und frauengerechtes Planen und Bauen, Md-Stadtbaudirektion.

— (2000), *„Die lungern eh' nur da rum'. Eine Betrachtung des Aufenthaltes von Jugendlichen der zweiten Generation aus der Türkei im öffentlichen Raum.* Diploma work, Universität Wien.

Grzinic, Marina and Reitsamer, Rosa (eds.), (2008), *New Feminism. Worlds of Feminism, Queer and Networking Conditions.* Wien: Löcker.

Guattari, Félix (1990), Ritornellos and Existential Affects, in *Discourse. Journal for Theoretical Studies in Media and Culture* 12.1, pp. 66 – 81.

Gürses, Hakan and Kogoj, Cornelia (eds.) (2004), *Gastarbajteri. 40 Jahre Arbeitsmigration.* Wien: Mandelbaum.

Hall, Stanley (1904), *Adolescence. Its Psychology and its Relations to Physiology, Anthropology, Sociology.* London – Sidney – New York: Appleton.

Hall, Stuart (1974), Black Men, White Media, in *SAVACOU, Journal of the Caribbean Artists Movement*, vol 9/10. Cited in Revealed: How UK media fuelled race prejudice. Chronicle World: changing Black Britain. http://www.chronicleworld.org/archive/issue_08/html_08/8_6_1rev.htm

Hannerz, Ulf (2004 [1969]), *Soulside. Inquiries into ghetto culture and community.* Chicago: The University of Chicago Press.

Hasaltay, Muzaffer (2007), *Der Freund*. 12 min short film. Video Edition Austria, medienwerkstatt. Release 02 (2009).

Hebdige, Dick (1991 [1979]), *Subculture. The Meaning of Style*. London: Routledge.

Helfferich, Cornelia (1994), *Jugend, Körper und Geschlecht. Die Suche nach sexueller Identität*. Opladen: Leske und Budrich.

Hillmann, Karl-Heinz (2007), *Wörterbuch der Soziologie*. 5. Auflage. Stuttgart: Alfred Kröner Verlag.

Hoffmann-Axthelm, Dieter (1995), Das Einkaufszentrum. In Fuchs, Moltmann, and Prigge (eds.), pp. 63 – 72.

Hurrelmann, Klaus (2006), *Einführung in die Sozialisationstheorie*. 9. Auflage. Weinheim und Basel: Beltz Verlag.

Ivekovic, Rada (2008), French Suburbia in 2005: The Return of the Politically Unrecognized. In Grzinic and Reitsamer (eds.), pp. 172 – 179.

Jacobs, Jane (1993 [1961]), *The Death and Life of Great American Cities*. New York: Random House.

Jeschke, Anna Laura (2000), *Einfach – Mehrfach 5. Temporäre Freiräume für Margareten*. Diploma work, Universität für Bodenkultur, Wien.

Kato, Masahide T. (2007), *From Kung Fu to Hip Hop. Globalization, Revolution, and Popular Culture*. Albany: State University of New York Press.

Khan, Verity Saifullah (1979), The Pakistanis: Mirpuri Villagers at Home and in Bradford. In Watson (ed.), pp. 57 – 89.

Khittel, Stefan, Plankensteiner, B. and Six-Hohenbalken, M. (eds.) (2004), *Contemporary Issues in Socio-Cultural Anthropology*. Wien: Löcker.

Larcher, Annelies (2007), „*Und dann schauen wir, wohin uns der Weg führt!" Freizeit im öffentlichen Stadtraum Wien aus der Perspektive von 14- bis 17-jährigen Mädchen*. Diploma work, Universität Wien.

Lepenies, Wolf (ed.) (1981), *Geschichte der Soziologie. Studien zur kognitiven, sozialen und historischen Identität einer Disziplin*. Frankfurt am Main: Suhrkamp.

Levine, Donald, Carter, Ellwood, and Gorman, Eleanor (1981), Simmels Einfluß auf die amerikanische Soziologie. In Lepenies, Wolf (ed.), pp. 32 – 81.

Liebow, Elliot (2003 [1967]), *Tally's Corner. A Study of Negro Streetcorner Men*. Lanham: Rowman&Littlefield.

Low, Setha M. (2000), *On the Plaza. The Politics of Public Space and Culture*. Austin: University of Texas Press.

Marcuse, Peter and van Kempen, Ronald (eds.) (2000), *Globalizing Cities. A New Spatial Order?* Oxford: Blackwell.

Mayer, Danila (1994), *Kurds' Migration from Central Anatolian Villages to Vienna – A Paradigm. A contribution to Urban Ethnology: Field Studies in Central Anatolia, Ankara, and Vienna*. Diploma work, Universität Wien.

— (1999), "Girls to Wolverhampton". Interview in Großegger, Heinzlmaier, and Zentner (eds.), pp. 160 – 166.

— (2005), Health Issues Among Viennese Marginalised Youth. Paper presented at World Congress on Health Challenges of the Third Millennium, International Forum for Social Sciences and Health, Istanbul.

—   (2007), Vienna Youth – Growing Up in a Multiethnic City. In Behera and
         Trawick (eds.), pp. 106 – 117.
—   (2008), Vienna Street Heroes. Black Music in Parks. Paper presented in
         workshop "Urban marginalization and popular culture", EASA Ljubljana.
         Electronic document, available online: http:// www.nomadit.co.uk/easa/
         easa08/panels.php5?PanelID=378.
—   (2009), Young Urban Migrants Between Two Cultures. In Prato (ed.), pp.
         151 – 172.
—   (2009) Urban Youth in Poverty: Physical Immobility and Virtual Real-
         ity. Some Observations from Vienna. Paper presented at Conference The
         Urban Poor: Mobilities and Mobilizations, Leiden University, Institute of
         Cultural Anthropology and Development Sociology.
—   (2010), "We're Doing It in the Park!" Park Youth in Vienna. A Contribution to
         the Anthropology of Urban Youth. Dissertation, Universität Wien.
Mayer, Danila and Möderndorfer, Christoph (Back on Stage 5) (1998), Jugendliche im
         öffentlichen Raum – Wien, Margareten. Wien: Österreichisches Institut für
         Jugendforschung (Austrian Institute for Youth Research).
McKenna, Terence (1999 [1992]), Food of the Gods. The Search for the Original Tree
         of Knowledge. A Radical History of Plants, Drugs and Human Evolution. 5th
         printing. London: Rider, Random House.
Mead, Margaret (1936 [1928]), Coming of Age in Samoa. A Psychological Study of Primi-
         tive Youth for Western Civilisation. Foreword by Franz Boas. 10th printing.
         New York: Blue Ribbon Books (William Morrow).
Mead, Margaret and Wolfenstein, Martha (1970 [1955]) (eds.), Childhood in Contemporary
         Cultures. 11th printing. Chicago and London: The University of Chicago Press.
Mutsch, Ursula (2008), Empirisch-quantitative Erforschung des Internetnutzungsverhal-
         tens von Jugendlichen in Internetcafés. Diploma work, Universität Wien.
The New York Times in Der Standard (May 7th, 2007), Specialized Medicine For the
         Awkward Years.
Oehme, Andreas, Beran, Christina, and Krisch, Richard (2007), Neue Wege in der Bil-
         dungs- und Beschäftigungsförderung für Jugendliche. Wien: Wissenschaftli-
         che Reihe des Vereins Wiener Jugendzentren, Band 4.
Parkgeschichten. Literatur von Jugendlichen (2006), Verein Wiener Jugendzentren (ed.).
         Idee, Konzept und Redaktion: Back On Stage 5. Wien.
Phillips, Mike and Phillips, Trevor (1999 [1998]), Windrush. The Irresistible Rise of
         Multi-Racial Britain. London: Harper Collins.
Pichler, Adelheid (2000), Girls go guuurrrl …. Grrrls–Culture: Selbstinszenierung als
         identitätsstiftendes Übergangsritual zwischen Schule und Arbeitsmarkt. Eine
         Bestandsaufnahme zu feministischer Mädchenarbeit und Biographiekonstruk-
         tion junger Frauen in Österreich. Diploma work, Universität Wien.
Plomb, Fabrice (2001), Jugendliche – allergisch gegen Arbeit? In Bourdieu (ed.), pp.
         54 ff.
Prato, Giuliana (ed.) (2009), Beyond Multiculturalism. Views from Anthropology. Urban
         Anthropology, Vol. 2. Farnham: Ashgate.

Rakic, Zorica (2010), *Open the Door: Rap & Jugend in Bezug auf Jugendliche mit Migrationshintergrund in Wien.* Dissertation, Universität Wien.

Riepl, Barbara and Williamson, Howard (eds.) (2009), *Portraits of Peer Violence in Public Space. Experiences from Young People in Four Localities in Europe.* Contributions to Youth Research, Volume 11. Wien: Austrian Institute of Youth Research.

Rolnik, Suely (2006), The Geopolitics of Pimping. European Institute for Progressive Cultural Policies 10/2006, translated by Brian Holmes. Electronic document, available online http://www.eipcp.net; www.transform.eipcp.net.

Rose, Tricia (1994), *Black Noise. Rap Music and Black Culture in Contemporary America.* Middletown: Wesleyan University Press.

Rotenberg, Robert (1995), *Landscape and Power in Vienna.* Baltimore: John Hopkins University Press.

Sansone, Livio (1995), The making of a black youth culture: lower-class young men of Surinamese origin in Amsterdam. In Amit-Talai and Wulff (eds.), pp. 114–143.

Sassen, Saskia (1995), Immigration in a World Economy. Paper presented at IFK workshop Migration and Uprooting of People. Vienna.

—   (2001) *The Global City. New York, London, Tokyo.* Princeton: Princeton University Press.

Scheper-Hughes, Nancy and Lock, Margaret L. (1998), The Mindful Body: A Prolegomenon to Future Work in Medical Anthropology. In Brown (ed.), pp. 208–224.

Schindlauer, Benjamin (2008), *Gesundheits- und Krankheitsverhalten von Jugendlichen mit Migrationshintergrund.* Diploma work, MedUni Wien.

Schlegel, Alice and Barry III, Herbert (1991), *Adolescence. An Anthropological Enquiry.* New York: The Free Press.

Schmidt, Andrea (2006), *Wer spielt verliert? Über das Gefahrenpotential von Glücksspielen in Wettbüros für Jugendliche.* Diploma work, FH Campus Wien.

Schomburg-Scherff, Sylvia M. (2001), Victor Witter Turner, in Feest and Kohl (eds.), pp. 485–492.

Schuster, Gudrun (1994), *Interkulturelle Kommunikation. Eine qualitative Studie über die Bedeutung des „Kulturkonfliktes" für Wiener Hauptschülerinnen aus deutschsprachigen, türkisch- und serbokroatischsprachigen Familien.* Diploma work, Universität Wien.

Sewell, Tony (1998), *Keep On Moving. The Windrush Legacy. The Black Experience in Britain from 1948.* London: Voice Enterprises.

Siegert, Sonja (2009), *Freizeitpädagogik und Kulturanthropologie: transkulturelle Beziehungen und Kompetenzen in der Parkbetreuung.* Dissertation, Universität Wien.

Sladen, Mark and Yedgar, Ariella (2007), *Panic Attack, Art in the Punk Years.* London – New York: Merrell.

Slama, Martin (2006), *Chatten in Indonesien. Eine sozialanthropologische Untersuchung über junge InternetuserInnen in einer multiplen Moderne.* Dissertation, University of Vienna.

—   (2010), The agency of the heart: internet chatting as youth culture in Indo-
         nesia. In Social Anthropology/Anthropologie Sociale. The Journal of the
         European Association of Social Anthropologists, Vol. 18, Number 3. Ox-
         ford: Blackwell Publishing Ltd., pp. 316 – 330.

The Social Science Encyclopedia (2004), Kuper, Adam and Kuper, Jessica (eds.). 3rd editi-
         on. London and New York: Routledge.

Southall, Aidan (1983), Towards a Universal Urban Anthropology. In Ansari and Nas
         (eds.), pp. 7 – 21.

—   (2000 [1998]), *The City in Time and Space*. Cambridge: Cambridge Univer-
         sity Press.

Stokes, Martin (1992), *The Arabesk Debate: Music and Musicians in Modern Turkey*. Ox-
         ford: Clarendon Press.

Streissler, Anna Isabella (1997), *"Tu no sabes lo que pueda pasar manana …". Eine ethno-
         logische Untersuchung zur Situation hispanischer Jugendlicher in La Soledad,
         Bogotá*. Diploma work, Universität Wien.

—   (2003) *Being Young, Becoming Citizens. Everyday life and political culture in two
         preparatory schools in Guadalajara, Mexico*. Dissertation, Universität Wien.

Swartz, Marc, Turner, Victor, and Tuden, Arthur (1976 [1966]), *Political Anthropology*.
         3rd printing. Chicago: Aldine.

Szatmary, David P. (1991 [1987]), *Rockin' In Time. A Social History of Rock-and-Roll*. 2nd
         printing. Englewood Cliffs: Prentice-Hall.

Thrasher, Frederic M. (1963 [1927]), *The Gang. A Study of 1,313 gangs in Chicago*.
         Abridged with a new Introduction by James F. Short. Chicago: The Univer-
         sity of Chicago Press.

Tönnies, Ferdinand, (1935 [1887]), *Gemeinschaft und Gesellschaft*. 8. Auflage. Leipzig:
         Hans Buske Verlag.

Tomasi, Luigi (ed.) (1999), *The Tradition of the Chicago School of Sociology*. Reprint. Al-
         dershot: Ashgate.

Toop, David (1994), *Rap Attack. African Jive bis Global Hip Hop*. München: Heyne.
         Translation: Diedrich Diederichsen.

Trawick, Margaret (2007), Cyberkids in Metropolitan America. In Behera and Trawick
         (eds.), pp. 194 – 210.

Turner, Victor W. (1994 [1974]), *Dramas, Fields, and Metaphors. Symbolic Action in Hu-
         man Society*. 7th printing. Ithaca – London: Cornell University Press.

Van Gennep, Arnold (2005 [1909]), *Übergangsriten (Les rites de passage)*. 3rd printing.
         Frankfurt – New York: Campus Verlag.

Verein Jugendzentren der Stadt Wien (ed.) (1999), *Sozialpädagogik und Jugendarbeit im
         Wandel. Auf dem Weg zu einer lebensweltorientierten Jugendförderung*. Wien:
         Wissenschaftliche Reihe des Vereins Jugendzentren der Stadt Wien, Band 1.

Wächter, Natalia (2004), *Doing gender & Doing ethnicity. Eine Untersuchung der Interak-
         tion von jugendlichen MigrantInnen in Chatrooms*. Dissertation, Universität
         Wien.

—   (2006), *Wunderbare Jahre? Jugendkultur in Wien. Geschichte und Gegenwart*.
         Weitra: Verlag Bibliothek der Provinz.

Wambu, Onyekachi (ed.) (1999), *Empire Windrush: Fifty Years of Writing About Black Britain*. London: Phoenix.

Ward, Brian (1998), *Just My Soul Responding. Rhythm and Blues, Black Consciousness, and Race Relations*. Berkeley: University of California Press.

Watson, James L. (1979 [1977]), Introduction: Immigration, Ethnicity, and Class in Britain. In Watson (ed.), pp. 1–20.

Whyte, William Foote (1943), *Street Corner Society. The Social Structure of an Italian Slum*. Chicago: The University of Chicago Press.

Die Wiener Break Dance Story, Video (2010), Leonhard Plakolm/Georg Rudolf. Wien: Verein Wiener Jugendzentren.

Wildner, Kathrin (2003), *Zócalo – Die Mitte der Stadt Mexico. Ethnographie eines Platzes*. Berlin: Dietrich Reimer Verlag.

Wilson, Peter Lamborn, Media Creed for the Fin De Siecle, electronic document, available online: www.hermetic.com/bey/pw-creed.html (accessed March 7th, 2011).

Wolf, Eric (2010 [1982]), *Europe and the People Without History*. 3rd edition with a New Foreword by Thomas Hylland Eriksen. Berkeley et al.: University of California Press.

Wolfenstein, Martha (1970), French Parents Take Their Children to the Park. In Mead and Wolfenstein (eds.), pp. 99–117.

Wollner, Eveline (1996), *Auf dem Weg zur sozialpartnerschaftlich regulierten Ausländerbeschäftigung in Österreich*. Diploma work, Universität Wien.

Wulff, Helena (1995), Inter-racial friendship: consuming youth styles, ethnicity and teenage femininity in South London. In Amit-Talai and Wulff (eds.), pp. 63–80.

Yu, Henry (2001), *Thinking Orientals: Migration, Contact, and Exoticism in Modern America*. Oxford: Oxford University Press.

Websites

Back on Stage, Einrichtungen der Mobilen Jugendarbeit (basic information, pictures, background texts, project and annual reports) http://www.mobilejugendarbeit.at

Okto Television http://www.okto.tv

Stadt Wien (City of Vienna) http://www.wien.gv.at

Verein Wiener Jugendzentren (information in English, reading for experts, pedagogic directrices, manuals, reports and studies, statistics) http://www.jugendzentren.at

Verein Wiener Sozialprojekte (Ganslwirt, Streetwork, CheckIt, and other drug social work projects) http://www.vws.or.at

Index